WITHDRAWN

2 95/5

25-71

FACTS ABOUT
CURRENT ENGLISH USAGE

THE NATIONAL COUNCIL OF TEACHERS OF ENGLISH

211 WEST SIXTY-EIGHTH STREET, CHICAGO, ILLINOIS

OFFICERS FOR 1938	EXECUTIVE COMMITTEE FOR 1938
President, MARQUIS E. SHATTUCK	DORA V. SMITH
1st Vice-President, ESSIE CHAMBERLAIN	CHARLES SWAIN THOMAS
2nd Vice-President, E. A. CROSS	HOLLAND D. ROBERTS
Secretary-Treasurer, W. WILBUR HATFIELD	And the OFFICERS of the Council

PUBLICATIONS

Issued by special committees of the National Council of Teachers
of English under the direction of the Publications Committee:
Stella S. Center   John J. DeBoer   Homer A. Watt
Neal M. Cross   Holland D. Roberts, *Chairman*

Reading for Fun (elementary book list)
Compilation directed by Eloise Ramsey

Books for Home Reading (for High Schools)

Leisure Reading (for Grades Seven, Eight, and Nine)
Compilations directed by Stella S. Center and Max J. Herzberg, Committee Co-Chairmen

Good Reading (for Colleges)
Compilation directed by Atwood H. Townsend, Committee Chairman

Current English Usage, Sterling Andrus Leonard, Committee Chairman

Guide to Play Selection, Milton Smith, Committee Chairman

The Teaching of College English, Oscar James Campbell, Committee Chairman

Photoplay Appreciation in American High Schools, William Lewin, Committee Chairman

An Experience Curriculum in English, W. Wilbur Hatfield, Committee Chairman

A Correlated Curriculum, Ruth Mary Weeks, Committee Chairman

Teaching High School Students to Read, Stella S. Center and Gladys L. Persons

Film and School, Helen Rand and Richard Lewis

Facts About Current English Usage, Albert H. Marckwardt and Fred G. Walcott

---

OFFICIAL ORGAN

The English Journal: College and High School Editions
Editor, W. Wilbur Hatfield, 211 West Sixty-Eighth Street, Chicago, Illinois

FACTS ABOUT
CURRENT ENGLISH USAGE

BY

ALBERT H. MARCKWARDT

AND

FRED G. WALCOTT

INCLUDING A DISCUSSION OF CURRENT USAGE
IN GRAMMAR FROM "CURRENT ENGLISH USAGE"

BY

STERLING A. LEONARD

A PUBLICATION OF
THE NATIONAL COUNCIL OF TEACHERS OF ENGLISH

———

APPLETON-CENTURY-CROFTS, INC.

NEW YORK

183256

39-919

COPYRIGHT, 1938, BY
THE NATIONAL COUNCIL OF TEACHERS OF ENGLISH

*All rights reserved. This book, or parts
thereof, must not be reproduced in any
form without permission of the publisher.*

6114-11

PE
1111
L4376
m3

PRINTED IN THE UNITED STATES OF AMERICA
E 59769

PREFACE

This study, which the Publications Committee of the National Council of Teachers of English has generously consented to make available in printed form, had its inception in two papers presented before the Current Language Problems section of the National Council of Teachers of English. In 1933, the year after the appearance of *Current English Usage,* Mr. Walcott read a paper entitled, "Some Practical Aspects of the Leonard Monograph" at the Council meeting held in Detroit. Mr. Marckwardt's paper was read at the Buffalo meeting in 1937. Both papers had the same end in view and employed the same technique. The authors collected evidence as to the usage of certain expressions for the purpose of comparing this evidence with the collected opinion in the Leonard report about the same expressions.

Thus it seemed feasible to combine the two papers into a single comprehensive study which would present the factual evidence concerning all, or nearly all, of the expressions surveyed in *Current English Usage.* It is this combination which is presented here. Mr. Walcott is responsible for the work on those items which both groups of judges voted "established." The items which were voted "established" by the linguists and "disputable" by the per-capita vote of all the judges were studied independently by both collaborators, the results being combined in this monograph. The work on the remaining "disputable" and the "illiterate" items was done by Mr. Marckwardt.

To help those readers who are not familiar with the original Leonard report, and to furnish a convenience for those who may wish to compare Leonard's findings with ours, the grammar portion of the Leonard study has been appended to this monograph.

A. H. M.

F. W.

CONTENTS

CURRENT USAGE IN GRAMMAR
Reprinted from
Current English Usage by Sterling A. Leonard

FACTS ABOUT
CURRENT ENGLISH USAGE

❧ I ❧

THE LEONARD STUDY ON USAGE

It was most appropriate that the first of the *English Monographs* sponsored by the National Council of Teachers of English should have dealt with the very fundamental problem of language. This monograph, *Current English Usage,* is the result of a study initiated by the late Professor Sterling A. Leonard. It was completed after his untimely death by a committee of the National Council and published in 1932. Appearing at a time when the researches of Leonard, Fries, and Pooley, to mention only a few, had established the unreliable character of the linguistic judgments in many school textbooks, this study sought to provide the classroom teacher with accurate and reliable information concerning English usage. The constant interest of the teaching profession in research of such a practical and helpful character is evidenced by the fact that the second printing of *Current English Usage* is now exhausted.

Although the appreciation of the teachers for this work has been manifest, there are two other aspects of its reception that deserve comment here. It should be recalled, first of all, that *Current English Usage* was the subject of much adverse journalistic comment both upon its initial appearance and when the second printing was issued. In general, these criticisms were either flippant or indignant; they seized upon what seemed to be some of the most startling of the findings and used them as a point of departure to predict the disintegration of the English language or to question the sanity of the authors. Almost without

exception the criticisms were neither penetrating nor constructive.

On the other hand, language scholars and language historians,
the individuals best qualified not only to make an intelligent ap-
praisal of the results of the Leonard study but to pursue some
of the stimulating problems that were raised in it, have given it
little notice. During the five years in which *Current English
Usage* has been available to them, there have been few studies
based upon it, and these deal with the pedagogical rather than
the linguistic implications of the study. It is, in part at least, the
purpose of this monograph to demonstrate the possibilities of
linguistic analysis of the *Current English Usage* results.

THE TECHNIQUE OF THE LEONARD STUDY

Before proceeding, it will be pertinent, however, to recall a
few of the details concerning the development of this study, the
method pursued by Leonard and his associates, and the results
which they presented. The study appears in what may be called
its initiatory stage in an article by Leonard and Moffett, entitled
"Current Definitions of Levels in English Usage," and published
in the *English Journal* for May, 1927 (pages 345–359). The purpose of the study is set forth in the following statement which
appears at the outset of the article:

This study was an attempt to find out what various judges have
observed about the actual use or non-use by cultivated persons of a
large number of expressions usually condemned in English textbooks
and classes.

The monograph *Current English Usage,* which appeared five
years later, was an enlargement of this earlier project, employing
the same method and having the same purpose in view. The first
significant fact to remember, then, is that *Current English Usage*
deals primarily not with usage itself but with opinion about the

usage of words and expressions usually questioned or condemned in grammars and handbooks.

The following technique was employed in securing this "consensus of expert opinion": a list of 230 expressions "of whose standing there might be some question" [1] was submitted to a group of 229 judges, composed of thirty linguistic specialists, an equal number of editors, twenty-two authors, nineteen business men, and about 130 teachers of English and of speech.[2] The judges were asked to place the various expressions into one of the following three categories, according to their observation of what usage is rather than their opinion of what usage ought to be:

1. Formally correct English, appropriate chiefly for serious and important occasions, whether in speech or writing; usually called "Literary English"

2. Fully acceptable English for informal conversation, correspondence, and all other writing of well-bred ease; not wholly appropriate for occasions of literary dignity; "standard, cultivated colloquial English"

3. Popular or illiterate speech, not used by persons who wish to pass as cultivated, save to represent uneducated speech, or to be jocose; here taken to include slang or argot, and dialect forms not admissible to the standard or cultivated area; usually called "vulgar English," but with no implication necessarily of the current meaning of vulgar; "naif, popular, or uncultivated English" [3]

That the stipulation to "score according to your observation of what is actual usage rather than your opinion of what usage

---

[1] Quoted from the instructions to the judges.

[2] Of these, approximately fifty were college instructors belonging to the Modern Language Association; another fifty, including many teachers from the high schools and grammar grades, consisted of members of the National Council; the remaining thirty were teachers of speech. There were really two lists of questionable expressions; the first, of 102 items, was submitted to all of the judges. This was the original list compiled by Leonard and Moffett in 1927. A second ballot of 130 items was submitted only to the linguists and members of the National Council.

[3] There was also a fourth category, "trade or technical English" which was employed so infrequently that it assumed no importance in the final tabulations and is omitted from consideration here.

should be" was at times more honored in the breach than in the observance is indicated by such comments as, "I do not like *very amused";* "I dislike this, but rather because it is stylistically bad than because it is grammatically incorrect"; and *"One* is the proper form." [4]

After these various ratings had been tabulated, the results were presented in *Current English Usage* in two lists, the first, pages 168–175, giving the ranking of all the items according to the vote of the linguists is reproduced below. The second, pages 179–186, gave the ranking of all the items according to a per capita vote of the whole group of judges. Each of these lists was divided into three parts. Those items which the judges generally agreed upon as being either literary or cultivated colloquial English were labeled *established.* Those items which were generally agreed upon as being uncultivated or popular English were labeled *illiterate.* Finally, the expressions about which there was marked disagreement were placed in a middle group and labeled *disputable.*[5]

GRAMMATICAL USAGES AS RANKED BY LINGUISTS

A. ESTABLISHED USAGES

1. *A Tale of Two Cities* is *an* historical novel.
2. It was *I* that broke the vase, father.
3. Why *pursue* a vain hope?
4. *One* rarely enjoys *one's* luncheon when *one* is tired.
5. The invalid was able *partially to raise* his body.

---

[4] *Current English Usage,* pp. 107, 134, 153.
[5] Approval as formal or cultivated colloquial English by at least 75 per cent of the judges was required to place an item in the "established" group; disapproval by at least 75 per cent of the judges was required to place an item in the "illiterate" category. Hence "disputable" usages are those approved by more than 25 per cent but less than 75 per cent of the judges.

6. It *behooves* them to take action at once.
7. I *had rather* go at once.
8. *In this connection,* I should add . . .
9. This is a man . . . I used to know. (Omitted relative.)
10. You *had better* stop that foolishness.
11. Each person should of course bear *his or her* share of the expense.
12. Galileo discovered that the earth *moved.*
13. This hat is *not so* large as mine.
14. My position in the company was satisfactory from every *point of view.*
15. He toils *to the end that* he may amass wealth.
16. *In the case* of students who elect an extra subject, an additional fee is charged.
17. The defendant's case was *hurt* by this admission.
18. *I for one* hope he will be there.
19. This is the chapter *whose* contents cause most discussion.
20. *Under these circumstances* I will concede the point.
21. I have no prejudices, and *that* is the cause of my unpopularity.
22. You may ask *whomsoever* you please.
23. The honest person is to be *applauded.*
24. He stood *in front of* the class to speak.
25. *This much* is certain.
26. He did not do *as* well *as* we expected.
27. We *got home* at three o'clock.
28. He has no fear; nothing can *confuse* him.
29. There is *a* large *works* near the bridge.
30. *As regards the League,* let me say . . .
31. "You just had a telephone call." "Did *they* leave any message?"
32. I was attacked by one of *those* huge police dogs.
33. The women were *all dressed up.*
34. This was the *reason why* he went home.
35. This book is valueless, that one has more to recommend it. (Comma splice.)
36. Take two *cups* of flour.
37. *None* of them *are* here.
38. I *drove* the car around the block.
39. He doesn't do it *the way* I do.
40. The New York climate is *healthiest* in fall.

41. I felt I could walk no *further*.
42. One is not *fit* to vote at the age of eighteen.
43. Our catch was *pretty* good.
44. We have made some progress *along these lines*.
45. The catcher stands *back of* the home plate.
46. My colleagues and I *shall* be glad to help you.
47. I went immediately into the banquet room, *which* was, I found later, a technical error.
48. That will be *all right,* you may be sure.
49. We will *try and get* it.
50. We cannot discover *from whence* this rumor emanates.
51. I can hardly *stand* him.
52. Jane *was home* all last week.
53. I*'d like* to make a correction.
54. I've absolutely *got* to go.
55. We can expect the commission *to at least protect* our interests.
56. That's a dangerous curve; you'd better go *slow*.
57. There are some *nice* people here.
58. *Will* you be at the Browns' this evening?
59. Have you *fixed* the fire for the night?
60. I don't know *if* I can.
61. *In hopes of* seeing you, I asked . . .
62. *It* says in the book that . . .
63. If it *wasn't* for football, school life would be dull.
64. His attack on my motives made me *peevish*.
65. We *taxied* to the station to catch the train.
66. We *only* had one left.
67. My *viewpoint* on this is that we ought to make concessions.
68. Factories were *mostly* closed on election day.
69. He moves mighty *quick* on a tennis court.
70. He stopped to *price* some flowers.
71. He worked with much *snap*.
72. This room is *awfully* cold.
73. It is *me*.
74. *Who* are you looking for?
75. A treaty was concluded *between the four powers*.
76. *You* had to have property to vote, in the eighteenth century.
77. The kind of apples you mean *are* large and sour.
78. I have a *heap* of work to do.

79. I *felt badly* about his death.
80. The real *reason* he failed *was because* he tried to do too much.
81. Invite *whoever* you like to the party.
82. Drive *slow* down that hill!
83. Harry was a little shaver about *this* tall.
84. I didn't speak to my uncle by long distance; I couldn't *get through.*
85. *They* had numerous strikes in England.
86. I will go, *providing* you keep away.
87. I have *got* my own opinion on that.
88. He made a *date* for next week.
89. My father walked very *slow* down the street.
90. There *was* a bed, a dresser, and two chairs in the room.
91. They invited my friends and *myself.*
92. It is now *plain and evident* why he left.
93. I wish I *was* wonderful.
94. I've no doubt *but what* he will come.
95. What was the reason for *Bennett making* that disturbance?
96. *Can* I be excused from this class?
97. Haven't you *got through* yet?
98. *Everyone* was here, but *they* all went home early.
99. He *loaned* me his skates.
100. My *folks* sent me a check.
101. He came *around* four o'clock.
102. If it had been *us,* we would admit it.
103. They went *way* around by the the orchard road.
104. The banker *loaned* me $200 at 6%.
105. *Pikes* Peak is in Colorado.
106. The sailors *laid* out along the yards.
107. Is your insurance sufficient *coverage* for your house?

B. DISPUTABLE USAGES

108. That clock must be *fixed.*
109. My contention has been *proven* many times.
110. Sam, who was then in town, was with me *the three or four first* days.
111. *One* rarely likes to do as *he* is told.
112. He never works *evenings* or *Sundays.*

113. They have *gotten* a new car this year.
114. The Rock Island *depot* burned down last night.
115. Sitting *in back of* John, he said, "Now guess what I have."
116. I took it to be *they*.
117. *I guess* I'll go to lunch.
118. He went *right* home and told his father.
119. He could write *as well* or *better than* I.
120. I *expect* he knows his subject.
121. I *can't seem to* get this problem right.
122. I was pretty *mad* about it.
123. *Either* of these *three* roads is good.
124. You are older than *me*.
125. What are the chances of *them* being found out?
126. There is *a big woods* behind the house.
127. I know it to be *he*.
128. Do you *wish* for some ice cream?
129. Intoxication is *when* the brain is affected by certain stimulants.
130. *Neither* of your reasons *are* really valid.
131. He *dove* off the pier.
132. Trollope's novels have already begun to *date*.
133. Will you go? *Sure.*
134. He is *kind of silly,* I think.
135. I *will probably* come a little late.
136. That was the reason for *me leaving* school.
137. They *eat* (et) dinner at twelve o'clock.
138. I'll swear that was *him*.
139. Well, that's *going some*.
140. *Leave* me alone, or else get out.
141. Of two disputants, the *warmest* is generally in the wrong.
142. It was *good and cold* when I came in.
143. We have*n't but* a few left.
144. In the collision with a Packard, our car naturally got the *worse* of it.
145. I wouldn't have said that if I had thought it *would have* shocked her.
146. *Yourself* and your guests are invited.
147. The man was *very amused*.
148. Such *naif* actions seem to me absurd.
149. It seems to be *them*.

150. Everybody bought *their* own ticket.
151. *Say,* do you know who that is?
152. I suppose that's *him*.
153. I *can't help but* eat it.
154. *Aren't ('nt* or *rnt)* I right?
155. There is a row of beds with a curtain *between each bed*.
156. If I asked him, he would *likely* refuse.
157. John didn't do so *bad* this time.
158. Cities and villages are being stripped of all they contain *not only, but* often of their very inhabitants.
159. *Everybody's else* affairs are his concern.
160. It *don't* make any difference what you think.
161. I read in the paper *where* a plane was lost.
162. That boy's mischievous behavior *aggravates* me.
163. That stock market collapse left me *busted*.
164. Neither author nor publisher *are* subject to censorship.
165. Yes, our plan worked just *fine*.
166. The fire captain with his loyal men *were* cheered.
167. Don't get *these* kind of gloves.
168. The British look at this differently *than* we do.
169. *Most* anybody can do that.
170. It is *liable* to snow tonight.
171. They went in *search for* the missing child.
172. I suppose I'm wrong, *ain't* I?
173. John was *raised* by his aunt.
174. Martha *don't* sew as well as she used to.
175. He *most* always does what his wife tells him.
176. It *sure* was good to see Uncle Charles.
177. My experience on the farm helped me *some*, of course.
178. It's *real* cold today.
179. His presence was valueless *not only*, but a hindrance as well.
180. We don't often see sunsets *like* they have in the tropics.
181. I am older than *him*.
182. She leaped off *of* the moving car.
183. She *sung* very well.
184. It is only a little *ways* farther.
185. It looked *like* they meant business.
186. Do it *like* he tells you.
187. The child was weak, *due to* improper feeding.

C. UNCULTIVATED OR ILLITERATE USAGES

188. John *had awoken* much earlier than usual.
189. I have*n't hardly* any money.
190. The engine was hitting *good* this morning.
191. The dessert was made with *whip* cream.
192. Now just *where* are we *at?*
193. The kitten mews whenever it *wants in.*
194. A woman *whom* I know was my friend spoke **next.**
195. He *drunk* too much ice water.
196. *Reverend Jones* will preach.
197. All came except *she.*
198. The *party* who wrote that was a scholar.
199. My Uncle John, *he* told me a story.
200. He *begun* to make excuses.
201. I *calculate* to go soon.
202. This is *all the further* I can read.
203. That *ain't* so.
204. The *data is* often inaccurate.
205. He looked at me and *says* . . .
206. I must go and *lay* down.
207. *Ain't* that just like a man?
208. Both leaves of the drawbridge *raise* at once.
209. The people *which* were here have all gone.
210. I *have drank* all my milk.
211. *That there* rooster is a fighter.
212. The old poodle was *to no sense* agreeable.
213. One of my brothers *were* helping me.
214. I enjoy wandering *among* a library.
215. A light *complected* girl passed.
216. I want *for you to come* at once.
217. He won't *leave* me come in.
218. There was *a* orange in the dish.
219. It was dark when he *come* in.
220. You *was* mistaken about that, John.
221. I wish he *hadn't of* come.
222. *Hadn't* you *ought* to ask your mother?
223. My cold *wa'nt* any better next day.
224. If John *had of* come, I needn't have.

225. I had hardly *laid* down again when the phone rang.
226. He did *noble*.
227. Somebody *run* past just as I opened the door.
228. Just *set* down and rest awhile.
229. The neighbors took turns *setting* up with him.
230. They *swang* their partners in the reel.

Although it is not necessary here to consider the merits of the practice followed in the body of the Leonard monograph, that of giving special prominence to the rankings of the linguists, there is no doubt that the final results were somewhat complicated by the presentation of two rankings instead of one. However, the following chart attempts to combine in a single tabulation the two rankings given in *Current English Usage,* that of the group of linguistic experts, and the per capita vote of all the judges.

TABLE I

DISTRIBUTION OF RANKINGS IN THE CURRENT ENGLISH USAGE BALLOTS

I. Expressions rated "established" by both groups .... 71 items
IIa. Expressions rated "established" by the linguists and "disputable" by the vote of the whole group .... 36 items
IIb. Expressions rated "disputable" by the linguists and "established" by the vote of the whole group .... 6 items
IIc. Expressions rated "disputable" by both groups .... 64 items
IId. Expressions rated "disputable" by the linguists and "illiterate" by the vote of the whole group .... 10 items
IIe. Expressions rated "illiterate" by the linguists and "disputable" by the vote of the whole group .... 5 items
III. Expressions rated "illiterate" by both groups .... 38 items
Total   230 items

To sum up the matter very briefly, seventy-one of the 230 test expressions were rated as acceptable or established both by the vote of the linguists considered separately and by the per capita vote of all the judges. Likewise these two groups also agreed in condemning as illiterate thirty-eight of the total number. This accounts for 109 of the 230 expressions. The status of the remaining 121 expressions is left somewhat in doubt since either one group of judges or both groups were unable to come to any agreement about them.

THE PURPOSE AND METHOD OF THIS STUDY

At this point in our analysis of *Current English Usage* we come to the purpose of the present study. It has been pointed out that Leonard and his associates made a survey of opinion about usage rather than the facts of usage. This appeal to opinion may be said to have had decisive results in less than one-half of the cases submitted to the judges. Both of these considerations suggest an avenue for further study of the same material: a compilation of the recorded facts of usage concerning the same 230 expressions and a comparison of these facts with the collected opinions represented by the Leonard report.

The attitude of the compilers of the Leonard report as to the reliability of available collections of linguistic fact is not wholly clear. Although the *Oxford Dictionary* and other dictionaries are frequently quoted in the detailed treatment of the various items, one finds in the introduction to the grammar section the following statement, justifying a survey of opinion rather than of fact:

Dictionaries have as their prime function the recording of usage, but by their very nature most of their citations have to be drawn from literary examples of acknowledged value; this method, valid though it may be, must of necessity result in a lag of several years between the adoption of a given usage and its appearance in a dictionary.[6]

On the other hand, the following excerpts from Leonard's original article indicate clearly enough that he intended his sur-

---

[6] *Current English Usage,* p. 95.

vey of opinion to be ancillary to, rather than a substitute for, a survey of fact.

1. The net result of the study is to make possible some interesting comparisons between (1) current statements by grammar and rhetoric texts, and particularly by the school of grammarians and rhetoricians which rose in the eighteenth century and has continued to this day, and (2) the record of actual cultivated usage as shown by this study, and by the complete dictionaries, particularly the Oxford.

2. It is submitted, however, that this record and that of the dictionary should help to set purists and their purism in a correct light.

3. In particular such data should be taken into account in deciding between the records of the dictionary-makers and those of the writers of textbooks whenever the latter purport to state what is actually used.[7]

It is, then, wholly in keeping with Leonard's conception of his survey to compare his findings, based on opinion, with available compilations of recorded usage, that is to say, recorded fact. The detailed treatments of the separate items in the body of *Current English Usage* do make such comparisons upon a great many occasions, but at the time this monograph was written neither the second edition of Webster's *New International Dictionary* nor the Supplement to the *Oxford Dictionary* was available. Moreover, information about a considerable number of the problems involved in the test expressions is not of a nature which lends itself to convenient or systematic presentation in a dictionary, but is, nevertheless, contained in other collections of linguistic fact.

It is particularly important to secure factual information about the status of the "disputable" expressions, those concerning which the survey of opinion gave an indecisive answer. It will be recalled that the judges—or the jury, properly speaking —disagreed in 121 cases out of 230. A jury disagreement is, of

---

[7] S. A. Leonard and H. Y. Moffett, "Current Definition of Levels in English Usage," *English Journal*, Vol. 16, May, 1927, pp. 356–359.

course, seldom a satisfaction or a help to any one, least of all to the teacher who is attempting to fashion his classroom practice on the basis of its findings. True enough, the Leonard study suggests in its conclusion that the teacher "will certainly, in marking themes, accept from the average student any usage classed in this study as established or disputable," [8] but in the very next sentence it is hinted that certain other usages may be more elegant than those labeled *disputable*. At any rate, the word *disputable* has a somewhat dubious sound and has no appropriate place in the description of usage, which is linguistic fact. A usage may be established; it may be popular; it may be regional; it may be upper or lower class; but strictly speaking, it cannot be disputable. Only opinion about it may be suitably described by such a term. When opinion fails to give a satisfactorily definite answer concerning the status of one or more expressions, the only thing that remains to be done, or that can be done, is to look at the facts.

The purpose of the present study, then, is to supplement the survey of opinion, which forms the basis of the Leonard monograph, with a survey of the recorded usage of the same 230 items. It has already been pointed out (1) that Leonard had no intention of excluding from consideration such a survey of fact; (2) that new sources of factual information have become available since the Leonard report was compiled; and (3) that in more than half the cases considered, the survey of opinion failed to give a decisive answer as to the status of the expressions. These considerations taken together seem to the authors to justify the present supplementary investigation.

THE METHOD IN THIS STUDY

Having outlined the purpose of the present study, one is immediately confronted with the problem of sources: What col-

---

[8] *Current English Usage*, p. 188.

lections of linguistic fact are to be employed in carrying it out? It will be accepted without argument, we believe, that the most convenient and authoritative single compilation of linguistic fact is the *Oxford Dictionary* together with its Supplement. Accordingly, the *Oxford Dictionary* was consulted in respect to each of the test expressions,[9] to discover what record there was of its use on the formal literary level, on the informal or colloquial level, in dialect, at the present time, or in any earlier period. In a great many instances the information given in the *Oxford Dictionary* was deemed sufficiently complete for the purposes of this investigation. Since this monumental work was a long time in the making, some of the earlier volumes are based on less complete evidence than those in the second half of the alphabet. Thus, it was felt desirable, at times, to add to the *Oxford Dictionary* data, information supplied by the second (1934) edition of Webster's *New International Dictionary*. This was especially true in the case of words or expressions whose status in usage is not the same in Great Britain and America. Horwill's *Modern American Usage*[10] was also consulted in respect to suspected Americanisms.

On a number of occasions the test expressions in the Leonard study were included for the purpose of presenting syntactical issues, as for example No. 141 in the linguists' ranking, which was designed to raise the question of the use of the superlative degree of an adjective in place of the comparative.[11] The essential point here is not the extent of the use of any single adjective in this fashion, but rather, usage in general in respect to this particular function of the adjective. In such instances the dictionary was not the most satisfactory source for a record of

---

[9] This statement stands in some need of qualification. In the portion of the investigation conducted by Walcott, namely the status of the "established" expressions, it was felt that to gather factual data concerning such unquestionably accepted expressions as "It is I," would be a work of supererogation.

[10] H. W. Horwill, *Modern American Usage* (Oxford, Clarendon Press, 1935).

[11] "Of two disputants, the *warmest* is generally in the wrong." *Current English Usage*, p. 139.

usage, and the grammars of Jespersen and Curme were used to supplement the dictionary findings.[12] These grammars have the weight of scholarly authority behind them, and in them illustrative citations from modern writings and from earlier periods are extensively employed to support the observations which are made. Likewise Hall's *English Usage*,[13] a record of usage based upon seventy-five thousand or more pages of literary English, was consulted at various points. In a few other instances articles in the scholarly journals were employed.

RESULTS OF THE INVESTIGATION

The results of this investigation may be most conveniently presented in condensed form, and a few words will suffice to explain the subsequent arrangement and treatment of the material. First of all, the 230 test expressions were divided into the three groups indicated in Table I ("established," "disputable," or "illiterate") on the basis of their combined rating in the two ballots. The authorities named previously were consulted in respect to each of these expressions. When the expression was found recorded in one or more of the collections of usages employed, it was placed in one of six categories, *Literary English, American Literary English, Colloquial English, American Colloquial English, Dialect,* or *Archaic.* The data concerning the expressions in each of the three groups were then combined. Since the record of usage in each of the groups, when compared with the Leonard survey of opinion, raises a number of questions and presents certain problems somewhat peculiar to itself, the three groups are considered separately in this study.

A few explanatory comments about the method of classification are in order here also. If the expression was recorded with-

---

[12] O. Jespersen, *A Modern English Grammar* (Heidelberg, 1928–31), 4 vols. G. O. Curme, *Syntax* (Boston, D. C. Heath and Co., 1931).
———, *Parts of Speech and Accidence* (Boston, D. C. Heath and Co., 1935).
[13] J. Leslie Hall, *English Usage* (Chicago, Scott, Foresman and Co., 1917).

out a limiting label in the collections of usage consulted, and if there was at least one citation from the nineteenth century, the expression was considered *Literary English*. The *Oxford Dictionary*, extensive as it is, found it necessary to limit the number of citations to one for each century—although in some cases more were used—and all of the volumes through the letter *I* had appeared by 1900. On the other hand, most of the nineteenth-century citations found were well within the second half of the century, so that there is little danger of an archaism being recorded here as in present use.

It must be admitted, of course, that if the last *Oxford Dictionary* citation for a certain expression happens to be 1875, a critic of this study might point out that usage could have changed in the last sixty years, that what was acceptable English in 1875 might have become unpalatable in the second quarter of the twentieth century. This is entirely possible, yet one or two considerations may be brought forward in defence of the procedure adopted here. First, if we may anticipate our results somewhat, the great majority of the supposed errors included in the test items were discovered, upon examination, to be usages which had been in the language for centuries, a number of them going back to the very beginnings of recorded English. To take a specific instance, the use of *between* referring to more than two (for example, A treaty was concluded *between* the *four* powers) is recorded in literary usage as early as 971, while the last citation given is 1885. While it is possible that the last fifty years might have seen a change in the status of this use of *between*, yet its continuous history of nine hundred years' standing would seem to militate against this supposition. It should be remembered also that the *Oxford Dictionary* editors had many more citations for most words than they could possibly use, and that citations were selected for inclusion upon considerations other than date. Thus if the last citation for a word bears the date 1875, this does not necessarily indicate that it is the most recent one that the editor had in his possession; it is merely the one he chose to have printed.

To return to the bases of classification, if an expression was given in any of the sources with the limiting label *U. S.* and the citations illustrating it were drawn from serious or formal writing, it was classified as *American Literary English*. The categories *Colloquial English* and *American Colloquial English* are self-explanatory. It must be emphasized, however, that the term *colloquial*, as it is employed in reputable dictionaries and by sound scholars, is not used in a derogatory sense. It merely means that the expression or word is to be found in spoken or informal written rather than in formal written English.

This division of items into *Literary English* and *American Literary, Colloquial English* and *American Colloquial* is incomplete in one respect. There is no provision for those usages which are peculiarly British English, since it should be assumed that the unqualified terms *Literary English* and *Colloquial English* imply acceptability on both sides of the Atlantic. However, since only three of the 230 items turned out to be Briticisms, the authors felt that a separate category for these would scarcely be necessary.

The *Dialect* category needs but one bit of explanation. Since the *Oxford Dictionary* recorded only dialectical words or expressions that had formerly been in general use, not those that had begun as dialect and remained so, the same qualification must apply to what is listed as dialect here. Any words or expressions for which no citations after 1800 were found in the *Oxford Dictionary* were listed as *Archaic* unless one of the other sources indicated that they were still in present use. If a word was labeled both *dialect* and *archaic* by the dictionaries, it was placed in the *dialect* category on the ground that it was still in use somewhere at the present time.

In contrast to the Leonard survey, which is based wholly and frankly upon subjective impression, the present authors have attempted to make their analysis as objective as possible. In general, the facts have been allowed to speak for themselves. The subjective element enters in only when the item under consideration is placed in one of the various categories, *Literary English, Dialect,* etc., and here it was occasionally necessary to differ with the conclusions reached by the dictionary editors and grammarians. If an expression was recorded without comment, but the citations appeared to have been drawn from informally written material or from dialogue, it was recorded as *Colloquial.* If, on the other hand, an expression was labeled *Colloquial* but the citations were chiefly drawn from works of a serious literary nature, the authors felt justified in classifying such an item as *Literary English.* In the case of disagreement among the various authorities, the only feasible solution seemed to be to classify the expression on the basis of the citations that were given.

In a few instances, notably those of *like* as a conjunction and *whoever* used obliquely, the dictionaries commented that although the expression was condemned by some, it was nevertheless to be found in many recent writers of standing. Because of this very definite statement concerning extent of usage, the only consistent policy in such cases seemed to be to assign the expressions to the literary category. The authors felt that the reported facts of usage deserved greater consideration than the reported attitude toward the expression. Likewise dictionary judgments as to grammatical correctness were considered of less weight than statements concerning extent of use; the former are frequently omitted from our direct quotations from the dictionaries.

Before proceeding to the detailed analysis of our findings one more thing remains to be said. In some respects the results of this study differ from certain widely held notions about present-day English to an even greater extent than the Leonard report. Therefore, it is possible that our work will meet with much of the same criticism that greeted the appearance of *Current English Usage*. The authors wish to make it clear at this point that in this study they are not advocating any one usage, a group of usages, or a level of usage. With advocacy of any kind we have absolutely no concern. We are only reporting the facts of the English language as they appear in the work of universally recognized authorities. We have conscientiously given all of the sources of our information so that our findings may be verified. The subjective element has been eliminated as far as was humanly possible, that is except for placing the items into their respective categories, and in performing this task we have attempted to lean neither to right nor left.

Moreover, it should be understood that the question of usage as a proper basis for grammar does not at all enter into this study, which concerns itself only with collecting the record of usage of a given number of items. Incidentally, these items were not chosen by the present authors. Nor are we attempting to fix as standard usage or to disguise as current English the occasional errors of one or a number of authors. In the first place, the term *error* implies a judgment based upon an already accepted standard, something quite outside the scope of our study. In the second place, the responsibility of recording the occasional error or supposed slip rests with the authorities we employed, not with us. Our only concern is to compare the evidence of language usage as it appears in the monuments of scholarship esteemed by all of us with the impressions of Leonard's judges, and to see what may be learned from such a comparison.

III

THE "ESTABLISHED" USAGES

The seventy-one items in the Leonard monograph which received a vote of "established" both in the ballot of the linguists and the per capita vote of the whole group are as follows: Nos. 1, 2, 3, 4, 5, 6, 7, 8, 9, 10, 11, 12, 13, 14, 15, 16, 17, 18, 19, 20, 21, 22, 23, 24, 25, 26, 28, 31, 32, 33, 34, 36, 38, 39, 40, 41, 42, 43, 44, 45, 46, 47, 48, 51, 52, 53, 54, 55, 56, 57, 58, 59, 60, 63, 64, 65, 70, 71, 72, 76, 77, 80, 83, 84, 85, 99, 103, 104, 105, 106, 107.[14]

Of the seventy-one established items, nine may be either classed as hyper-urbanisms, or else they are such as would seem to conform to the traditional standard of grammatical correctness to the extent of being almost non-controversial. That these nine expressions should be intermingled with the other items might be considered somewhat ill advised anyway, for any judgments concerning them entail for the most part a reversal of the critical issue, from proscribing what might appear as questionable to disapproving what might seem too fastidious. The nine examples follow in their numerical order:

1. *A Tale of Two Cities* is *an* historical novel.
2. It was *I* that broke the vase, father.
4. *One* rarely enjoys *one's* luncheon when *one* is tired.
5. The invalid was able *partially to raise* his body.
6. It *behooves* them to take action at once.

---

[14] The numbering here is based on the ranking given the item in the vote of the linguists; the same scheme was used in the body of *Current English Usage*.

11. Each person should of course bear *his or her* share of the expense.

13. This hat is *not so* large as mine.

22. You may ask *whomsoever* you please.

46. My colleagues and I *shall* be glad to help you.

It is perhaps sufficient to note that 72 per cent of all the judgments upon these nine items fall within the literary category; 23 per cent class them as colloquial; and only 5 per cent brand them as illiterate.[15] Surely these are not questions of active controversy, nor are they of immediate concern to teachers of English expression.

A similar group may also be tentatively distinguished from the class of "usually condemned" usages; they represent shades of distinction entirely too subtle for any but the more fastidious of literary stylists to differentiate. The list follows:

3. Why *pursue* a vain hope?

8. *In this connection,* I should add . . .

14. My position in the company was satisfactory from every *point of view.*

15. He toils *to the end that* he may amass wealth.

16. *In the case* of students who elect an extra subject, an additional fee is charged.

17. The defendant's case was *hurt* by this admission.

18. *I for one* hope he will be there.

20. *Under these circumstances* I will concede the point.

21. I have no prejudices, and *that* is the cause of my unpopularity.

23. The honest person is to be *applauded.*

24. He stood *in front of* the class to speak.

25. *This much* is certain.

28. He has no fear; nothing can *confuse* him.

---

[15] These percentages are derived by adding together the total number of opinions upon this entire group of items that fall within each of the three respective categories: literary, colloquial, and illiterate English; and then dividing each of the three totals by the entire number of judgments passed upon the composite group. The figures are not offered with any mistaken notion of precise mathematical proportions. They merely reflect a fairly accurate summary of the general attitudes of the judges toward the composite group which we have chosen to consider separately.

32. I was attacked by one of *those* huge police dogs.

44. We have made some progress *along these lines.*

45. The catcher stands *back of* the home plate.

47. I went immediately into the banquet room, *which* was, I found later, a technical error.

48. That will be *all right,* you may be sure.

64. His attack on my motives made me *peevish.*

Here we have nineteen items that can scarcely be said to involve grammatical problems at all. The printed comments upon them are significant of this. The collective tabulations in the case of this group are again significant. The judges divide, for the most part, between placing them in the accepted literary category (38.4 per cent) or in the cultivated colloquial group (54.9 per cent). Only 6.7 per cent of all the judges' opinions upon these respective items would place them definitely within the class of illiterate expression. The ultra-stylistic nature of these problems, together with the significant expression of the judges upon them, should surely establish the group as relatively unimportant for classroom emphasis.

There is still another class of usage that is admittedly technical, usage that has become current in some specialized department of affairs and that the literary writer must almost of necessity adopt whenever he would invade the new field of denotations. The editors place four items of the seventy-one within this special class.[16]

104. The banker *loaned* me $200 at 6 per cent.

105. *Pikes* Peak is in Colorado.

106. The sailors *laid* out along the yards.

107. Is your insurance sufficient *coverage* for your house?

---

[16] It it interesting to note that of these four items the judges recognized only the last as definitely established in technical use. The editors, after remarking the general misunderstanding occasioned by Nos. 104 and 106, arbitrarily included these two within the established group *on the authority of the dictionaries,* and contrary, in the case of the latter item at least, to the overwhelming opposition of the judges.

There are also some other expressions that might be called *colloquially technical*—that is, they have come to represent meanings in colloquial use for which satisfactory literary substitutions are superfluous, if not impossible. The following usages may be classified in this fashion:

36. Take two *cups* of flour.
38. I *drove* the car around the block.
65. We *taxied* to the station to catch the train.
84. I didn't speak to my uncle by long distance; I couldn't *get through*.

The judges are very tolerant of these four usages. When they are taken collectively, 12.7 per cent of all the opinions are for inclusion within the literary category, as against 6.9 per cent for the illiterate. The greater proportion of the judgments, 80.4 per cent, place them within the cultivated colloquial group.

We have now reduced the list of seventy-one "established" usages to thirty-five items about which a considerable portion of our more active language controversies are likely to arise. The major aim of the present section of this study will be to consider this group of thirty-five language problems from the point of view of actual evidence of usage, either literary or colloquial, in order to substantiate or to refute the findings of the questionnaire by material proof.

The evidence in respect to the use of each of these items is presented here in condensed form. In each case the expression is quoted in full with the point in question italicized; the ranking in the two *Current English Usage* ballots is given, the dates of the earliest and latest citations which have been found, and any additional information concerning the spheres or limitations of use is also given. It should be understood, also, that when certain authors are cited as using a particular locution, the evidence is not at all confined to the writers mentioned. We have merely selected representative names to give the reader a general idea of the range and extent of use. The letters at the extreme right margin following the resumé of evidence indicate the category in which the authors have placed the expression in question, as *Literary English, Colloquial English,* etc. It may be pointed out again that the application of such labels represents ultimately a subjective judgment, but that at all times the authors have conscientiously attempted to make this judgment depend on the evidence before them.

To facilitate reference to the evidence in the *Oxford Dictionary,* the number of the definition under which the particular use of the word or expression is treated has been given, immediately preceding the dates of the citations. In the case of forms of verbs, this practice could not be followed since such forms were frequently scattered throughout the treatment of the word.

KEY TO ABBREVIATIONS

L followed by a number indicates the ranking in the ballot of the linguists (see pages 4–12).

WG followed by a number indicates the ranking in the ballot of the whole group of judges.

OD—Oxford Dictionary

OD Sup—Oxford Dictionary Supplement

Jesp—Jespersen, *Modern English Grammar* (quoted by volume and page)

Curme PSA—Curme, *Parts of Speech and Accidence*

Hall EU—Hall, *English Usage*

Pooley—Pooley, *Grammar and Usage in Textbooks on English*

LE—Literary English

ALE—American Literary English

CE—Colloquial English

ACE—American Colloquial English

Dial—Dialect

Arch—Archaic

ESTABLISHED USAGES

L 7: WG 30. I *had rather* go at once.   **LE**
   OD, s.v. *rather* adj. 9 d, 1450–1875.
Jesp III, 35, cites Defoe, Thackeray, Shaw, Wells.
Hall EU, 116–121, names 32 authors who use it.

L 9: WG 19. This is a man . . . I used to know.   **LE**
   (Omitted relative.)
   Jesp III, 133, cites examples from 906
to present time.

L 10: WG 28. You *had better* stop that foolishness.   **LE**
   OD, s.v. *better* 4 b, 971–1875, including
Shakespeare.

L 12: WG 29. Galileo discovered that the earth
   moved.   **LE**
   Jesp IV, Chap. XI, cites Chaucer, Shakespeare, Bunyan, Defoe, Franklin, Goldsmith, Boswell, Hunt, Dickens, Shaw, Bennett, Wilde, Galsworthy, and Barrie.

L 19: WG 22. This is the chapter *whose* contents
   cause most discussion.   **LE**
   OD, 3, 1382–1896, including Shakespeare
and Milton. *Jesp III,* 129, cites Marlowe, Shakespeare, Shelley, Stevenson, and others. *Hall EU,*
320–327, lists 150 authors, from Malory to present
day, who use the expression.

L 26: WG 33. He did *not* do *as* well *as* we expected.   **LE**
   Storm, *Englische Philologie,* 696, cites
Swift, Johnson, Boswell, Burney, Dickens, Marryat,
Trollope, and others.

L 31: WG 58. "You just had a telephone call."
   "Did *they* leave any message?"   **LE**
   OD, 2, 3, 1415–1896. *Jesp III,* 137, "fre-
quent." Cites Thackeray.

L 33: WG 45. The women were *all dressed up.*   **LE**

   OD, s.v. *dress* vb. 7 d, 1674–1721. *Jesp III,* 330. *Webster* records without comment.

L 34: WG 49. This was the *reason why* he went home.   **LE**

   OD, s.v. *why* 5 a, 1225–1908.

L 39: WG 31. He doesn't do it *the way* I do.   **LE**

   OD, 14, 725–1897, cites Shakespeare, Addison, Hardy, and others.

L 40: WG 71. The New York climate is *healthiest* in fall.   **LE**

   OD, s.v. healthy 2, 1552–1871.

L 41: WG 50. I felt I could walk no *further.*   **LE**

   OD, adv. 1, 1000–1855. Curme, *Syntax,* 502: "In adverbial function *farther* and *further* are used indiscriminately." See also *Pooley,* 128–130.

L 42: WG 36. One is not *fit* to vote at the age of eighteen.   **LE**

   OD, adj. 4, 1573–1868, Shakespeare, Franklin, Browning, and others cited.

L 43: WG 34. Our catch was *pretty* good.   **LE**

   OD, adv. 1, 1565–1896. *Hall EU,* 217–219, cites 52 authors.

L 51: WG 54. I can hardly *stand* him.   **LE**

   OD, 59 a and b, 1626–1891, including Steele, Chesterfield, Carlyle. Two examples from Mrs. Oliphant used with reference to persons; the others are not.

L 52: WG 46. Jane was *home* all last week.   **CE**

   OD, adv. 2, 1587–1885, although it is doubtful whether any of the examples clearly obviate the sense of motion toward or result of motion toward. Curme, *Syntax,* 145, "popular speech."

L 53: WG 40. I'd *like* to make a correction. **LE**

> *Jesp IV*, 315, cites Thackeray, Kipling, Wilde, and D. H. Lawrence. Curme, *Syntax*, 368, cites Mrs. H. Ward.

L 54: WG 72. I've absolutely *got* to go. **LE**

> *OD*, s.v. *get*, 24, 1876–1889, Ruskin cited. *Jesp IV*, 51, cites Disraeli, Dickens, Eliot, Ruskin, Wilde, Shaw, Wells, Trollope. *Hall EU*, 121–123, cites 13 authors. *OD* labels this "colloq. or vulgar," but in view of the authors cited it is classified as *literary* here.

L 55: WG 48. We can expect the commission *to at least protect* our interests. **LE**

> Curme, *Syntax*, 458 ff., cites innumerable examples from the fourteenth century to the present. *Hall EU*, 266–275, cites 34 authors who use it.

L 56: WG 52. That's a dangerous curve; you'd better go *slow*. **LE**

> *OD*, adv. 1, 1500–1858, including Shakespeare, Milton, Byron, and Thackeray.

L 57: WG 41. There are some *nice* people here. **LE**
> *OD*, adj. 15, 1769–1897.

L 58: WG 42. *Will* you be at the Browns' this evening? **LE**

> *Jesp IV*, 255, "now increasingly frequent." C. C. Fries, "The Periphrastic Future with *Shall* and *Will* in Modern English," *Publications of the Modern Language Association*, XL (1925), 963 ff., finds in English drama from 1557 to 1915 a total of 505 cases of *will* to 7 of *shall* in second-person questions.

L 59: WG 47. Have you *fixed* the fire for the night? **ACE**

> *OD*, 14 b, 1769–1891, including Mar-

ryat, Holmes, comments "chiefly U.S. colloq." *Jesp III*, 244, "in US = 'repair.' "

L 60: WG 65. I don't know *if* I can.   **LE**

OD, conj. 9, *Beowulf*–1895, including Caxton, the *Bible*, and Dryden. *Jesp III*, 42, cites Shakespeare, Byron, and present-day authors.

L 63: WG 68. If it *wasn't* for football, school life would be dull.   **LE**

Jesp IV, 130, cites Marlowe, Spectator, Sheridan, Austen, C. Brontë in constructions with the negative. C. Alphonso Smith, "The Indicative in Unreal Condition," *Modern Philology*, V, 361, gives earliest examples from fifteenth-century *Battle of Otterburn* and follows with others from Pepys, Bunyan, Defoe, Burke, Sheridan, a host of nineteenth-century writers, and comments, "By no means confined to colloquial language."

L 70: WG 51. He stopped to *price* some flowers.   **LE**

OD, vb. 3, 1845–1872.

L 71: WG 69. He worked with much *snap*.   **LE**

OD, sb. 11, 1872–1894.

L 72: WG 70. This room is *awfully* cold.   **CE**

OD, 3, 1816–1878, comments "slang," but examples are apparently colloquial rather than slang.

L 76: WG 57. *You* had to have property to vote, in the eighteenth century.   **LE**

OD, 6, 1577–1870. Bacon, Swift, and Ruskin cited.

L 77: WG 61. The kind of apples you mean *are* large and sour.   **CE**

OD, s.v. *kind*, sb. 14 b, 1382–1797, citing Wycliff and Shakespeare, comments "still common colloquially." *Jesp II*, 66, and Curme, *Syntax*, 544, label this construction colloquial.

L 80: WG 66.   The real *reason* he failed *was because* he tried to do too much.   **LE**

    OD, s.v. *because,* conj. 2, 1656, com-
ments *"Obs."* (common *dial.*). *Pooley,* 119, cites
the construction in speeches by Stuart Chase and
Curme, and in writings by Edith Franklin Wyatt,
Clarence Day, and Frank Harris. E. E. Ericson,
Anglia, 41 (1937), 112–113, cites Thomas Hobbes,
W. L. Phelps, W. P. Trent, John Macy, the New
York *Times,* and Baltimore *Sun.*

L 83: WG 14.   Harry was a little shaver about
this tall.   **LE**

    OD, adv. 2 b, 1460–1885.

L 85: WG 67.   *They* had numerous strikes in
England in 1860.   **CE**

    OD, 3, 1415–1896, Shakespeare and
Jonson cited. "Much used colloquially and dialectically."

L 99: WG 63.   He *loaned* me his skates.   **ALE**

    OD, vb., 1200–1901, but comments,
"Now chiefly U.S." *Hall EU,* 150–151. Horwill,
Modern American Usage, 192, "In America it is
still a verb." *Webster* records without comment.

L 103: WG 73.   They went *way* around by the orchard road.   **ACE**

    OD, adv. 2, 1849–1908, "obs. exc. Sc.,
north., and U.S." *Webster,* "dial. or colloq."

The detailed evidence which has been presented for the
thirty-five expressions in the "established" group which might
be considered at all controversial may be summarized in the
following manner:

1. Twenty-nine of the thirty-five moot usages appear to satisfy
most of the demands of formal literary English. These are as follows: Nos. 7, 9, 10, 12, 19, 26, 31, 33, 34, 39, 40, 41, 42, 43, 51,
53, 54, 55, 56, 57, 58, 60, 63, 70, 71, 76, 80, 83, 99.

2. Four of the usages, Nos. 52, 72, 77, and 85 are definitely restricted to colloquial and informal written English.

3. Two items, Nos. 59 and 103, appear to be in acceptable colloquial use in America but not in England.

The most significant aspect of these conclusions lies in the relatively few colloquialisms to be found in the "established" group. In compiling the results of the judges' ballots, Leonard and his associates counted as "established" those items which 75 per cent or more of the judges had marked as appropriate to formal literary *or* colloquial English. A survey of actual usage, however, shows that even of the thirty-five most dubious of the "established" items, only six are restricted to the colloquial or informal level. Thus we have our first inkling of the conservatism of opinion when compared with the recorded facts of usage.

❧ IV ☙

THE "DISPUTABLE" USAGES

It has already been remarked that those usages which the editors of the Leonard study labeled *disputable* are simply those about which the judges were unable to agree. To repeat, the appellative *disputable* is not appropriate in the description of a linguistic fact; it merely is an indication of the extreme variation of opinion. To illustrate, item No. 111 in the list, *"One rarely likes to do as he is told,"* was considered appropriate for formal literary usage by six linguists but illiterate by ten; on the other hand, thirty members of the Modern Language Association approved it for formal literary usage, whereas only two condemned it as illiterate. Along with several other items it ranked second in the vote of the English Council but thirty-third in the vote of the linguists. Obviously when opinions about acceptability vary to such an extent, it is not only important but absolutely essential to have recourse to the facts.

The evidence of usage as to the 121 disputable items is presented below; these items are considered in groups as indicated by the subdivisions of class II in Table I.

DISPUTABLE USAGES

A. LINGUISTS, "ESTABLISHED"; WHOLE GROUP "DISPUTABLE."

L 27: WG 79. We *got home* at three o'clock. CE
       OD, s.v. *get,* vb. 25, 1300–1712; s.v.
  home, adv. 7, 1806–1886. The citations appear to

be informal rather than literary even though they are recorded without comment.

L 29: WG 89. There is *a* large *works* near the bridge.   **LE**

OD, s.v. *work,* sb. 18, 1882–1898 (with the indefinite article), *Webster,* "often construed as a singular." *Jesp II,* 152, quotes Masefield (2) and Bennett.

L 30: WG 81. *As regards the League,* let me say. . . .   **LE**

OD, s.v. *regard,* vb. 7 c, 1824–1885. *Jesp III,* 178, characterizes this as a "frequent combination."

L 35: WG 89. This book is valueless, that one has more to recommend it. (Comma splice.)   **LE**

Naturally a problem such as the comma splice, which is the point of this expression, would not be treated in the sources employed. Summey, *Modern Punctuation,* 79, asserts that this punctuation "is manifestly growing in favor."

L 37: WG 84. *None* of them *are* here.   **LE**

OD, 2 b, 888–1887. The earliest instance with a plural verb is not 1580 as asserted in *Current English Usage,* 104.

L 49: WG 99. We will *try and get* it.   **LE**

OD, s.v. *try,* vb. 16 b, 1686–1883. This expression is labeled *colloquial* in the *OD* but the citations are drawn from reputable literary sources, including Milton and Coleridge. It is not so labeled in *Webster* where Milton's use of the expression is cited. *Hall EU,* 309, cites twenty-eight instances from ten authors.

L 50: WG 103. We cannot discover *from whence* this rumor emanates.   **LE**

OD, s.v. *whence,* 1377–1887.

L 61: **WG** 100. *In hopes of* seeing you, I
asked . . . .   LE

OD, s.v. *hope*, sb. 1 c, 1659–1702 (in
phrase given here). Plural of the substantive cited
as late as 1864. Recorded in *Webster* as present
usage.

L 62: **WG** 101. *It* says in the book that . . . .   CE

OD, 3 f, 1175–1482. Labeled "modern
colloquial." *OD Sup* has examples up to 1927.

L 66: **WG** 96. We *only* had one left.   LE

OD, adv. 1 c. 1483–1875, including
Dryden and Tennyson, with comment, "Frequent
in speech," but citations are definitely literary in
character. *Hall EU,* 187–193, gives a list of 400 instances from 104 authors to illustrate this construction.

L 67: **WG** 85. My *viewpoint* on this is that we
ought to make concessions.   LE

OD, a, 1856–1892.

L 68: **WG** 82. Factories were *mostly* closed on
election day.   LE

OD, citations with *mostly* in a position
comparable to this, 1594–1719; *mostly* with the
meaning in question is cited as late as 1904.

L 69: **WG** 93. He moves mighty *quick* on a tennis court.   LE

OD, adv. 1, 1290–1874, Shakespeare,
Milton, Tennyson, and others cited.

L 73: **WG** 124. It is *me*.   CE

OD, pron. 6, 1591–1758, Shakespeare
and Goldsmith cited. *Webster,* "colloquial and dialect."

L 74: **WG** 131. *Who* are you looking for?   CE

OD, pron. 5, 1450–1881, "common in
colloquial use." Shakespeare, Southey, and Hardy
cited.

L 75: **WG** 112. A treaty was concluded *between the four powers.*   LE

                    OD, s.v. *between,* prep. 19, 971–1885.

L 78: **WG** 104. I have a *heap* of work to do.   CE

                    OD, sb. 4, 1661–1884, "Colloq."

L 79: **WG** 88. I *felt badly* about his death.   Dial

                    OD, 7, 1783–1821, "Dial." *Webster,* "Dial."

L 81: **WG** 111. Invite *whoever* you like to the party.   LE

                    OD, 3, 1592–1780, including two quotations from Shakespeare. *Webster,* "common colloquially and *still found in good writers.*"

L 82: **WG** 97. Drive *slow* down that hill!   LE

                    OD, adv. 1, 1500–1858, Shakespeare, Milton, Byron, and Thackeray cited.

L 86: **WG** 105. I will go, *providing* you keep away.   LE

                    OD, b, 1632–1874.

L 87: **WG** 114. I have *got* my own opinion on that.   LE

                    OD, s.v. *get,* vb. 24, 1596–1878, "in familiar language." Shakespeare, Johnson, and Thackeray cited. *Jesp IV,* 48, "the 19th c. examples show its extension to higher forms of literature," citing among others Scott, Austen, Thackeray, Morris, Ruskin, Wilde, and Shaw. *Webster* records and cites Herbert.

L 88: **WG** 115. He made a *date* for next week.   ACE

                    OD Sup, sb.^{2} 2 c, 1896–1928, "U.S. colloq."

L 89: **WG** 83. My father walked very *slow* down the street.   LE

                    See L 82 above.

L 90: WG 121. There *was* a bed, a dresser, and two chairs in the room.   LE
> *Jesp II*, 181–182, 1470–1909. *Hall EU*, 53–58, gives examples from *Beowulf*, Malory, Shakespeare, *Bible*, Milton, Thackeray, and others.

L 91: WG 109. They invited my friends and *myself*.   LE
> *OD*, 3, 1205–1856, "in an enumeration, when not occupying first place . . . commonly preferred to *me*."

L 92: WG 106. It is now *plain and evident* why he left.   CE
> *OD*, s.v. *plain*, adj. 6, 1398: "openne and playne." *OD*, 6, 1729: "plain and easy to be understood." *OD*, 4, 1736: "plain and obvious." *Jesp II*, 373, "A variant form of adjective-subjunct is found in colloquial and dialectal speech when *and* is added between the two adjectives."

L 93: WG 113. I wish I *was* wonderful.   LE
> *OD*, s.v. *be*, vb. 7 ¶, 1684–1787. *Jesp IV*, 129, cites Defoe, Swift, Fielding, Austen, Byron, Marryat, Thackeray, Dickens, Hardy, Meredith, Wilde, Norris, and others.

L 94: WG 110. I've no doubt *but what* he will come.   CE
> *OD*, s.v. *but*, 30, 1662–1884, "dial. and colloq." The citations are colloquial rather than dialect.

L 95: WG 94. What was the reason for *Bennett making* that disturbance?   LE
> Curme, *Syntax*, 488, 1338–1925. *Hall EU*, 136–143, cites 217 instances in fifty-three authors.

L 96: WG 150. *Can* I be excused from this class?   LE
> *OD Sup*, vb.[1] B 6 b, 1894–1905, citing Hardy. Curme, *Syntax*, 411.

L 97: **WG** 122.   Haven't you *got through* yet?   **CE**
     OD, s.v. *get*, vb. 43, 1694–1895. Although no comment is made, the citations are chiefly colloquial in nature.

L 98: **WG** 78.   *Everyone* was here, but *they* all went home early.   **LE**
     OD, s.v. *every*, 10 c, 1735–1877, "The pronoun referring to *everyone* is often plural."

L 100: **WG** 90.   My *folks* sent me a check.   **CE**
     OD, 4, 1715–1833. The citations are colloquial in nature. *Webster*, "colloquial."

L 101: **WG** 107.   He came *around* four o'clock.   **ALE**
     OD Sup, prep. 4 b, 1888–1920, "U.S."

L 102: **WG** 135.   If it had been *us,* we would admit it.   **CE**
     OD, 5 d, 1883–1897, "Common in dialect and colloquial use, and occasionally employed in writing."

  B. LINGUISTS, "DISPUTABLE"; WHOLE GROUP, "ESTABLISHED."

L 108: **WG** 60.   That clock must be *fixed.*   **ACE**
     OD, vb. 14 b, 1769–1891, "chiefly U.S. colloq." *Jesp III*, 244, "in U.S. = repair."

L 109: **WG** 43.   My contention has been *proven* many times.   **LE**
     OD, s.v. *prove*, vb. A 2, 1536–1899, "properly in passive."

L 111: **WG** 16.   *One* rarely likes to do as *he* is told.   **LE**
     OD, pron. 21, 1607–1652. Curme, *Syntax,* 531. "The older forms *he, his, him,* still linger on." Galsworthy cited.

L 112: **WG** 55.   He never works *evenings* or *Sundays.*   **ALE**
     OD Sup, s.v. *evening,* d, 1862–1926, "chiefly U.S. and dialect."

L 114: **WG** 53. The Rock Island *depot* burned down last night.   ALE

OD, 5, 1830–1892, "U.S."

L 118: **WG** 56. He went *right* home and told his father.   ALE

OD, adv. 3 c, 1849–1901, "U.S."

C. BOTH GROUPS, "DISPUTABLE."

L 110: **WG** 120. Sam, who was then in town, was with me *the three or four first days.*   LE

OD, s.v. *first*, adj. 2 c (*a*), 1340–1781, "This still survives, though it is now rarely used when numbers above 3 or 4 are concerned." *Webster*, "may otherwise follow numbers."

L 113: **WG** 98. They have *gotten* a new car this year.   ALE

OD, 1868, "In U.S. literature *gotten* is still very common." *Webster*, "esp. in U.S."

L 115: **WG** 123. Sitting *in back of* John, he said, "Now guess what I have."   ACE

OD does not record expression with introductory preposition *in*. Curme, *Syntax*, 564, "popular American."

L 116: **WG** 125. I took it to be *they*.   Dial

OD, 1 b, 1380–1890, "now only dial. or illiterate." This statement is made without reference to the particular construction given here.

L 117: **WG** 108. *I guess* I'll go to lunch.   ACE

OD, vb. 6, 1692–1885, "colloquial in Northern U.S."

L 119: **WG** 118. He could write *as well* or *better than* I.

Not recorded.

L 120: WG 144. I *expect* he knows his subject.   **CE**

        OD, 6, 1592–1877, "Now rare in literary use." Curiously enough five examples are cited from the nineteenth century. The *OD* comments further, "is often cited as an Americanism but is very common in dialectal, vulgar, or carelessly colloq. speech in England." *Webster* "chiefly colloquial."

L 121: WG 102. I *can't seem to* get this problem right.   **LE**

        OD does not record; *Webster* records without comment.

L 122: WG 126. I was pretty *mad* about it.   **ACE**

        OD, 5, 1300–1867, "In many dialects in Great Britain and the U.S. the ordinary word for 'angry.'" *OD Sup* gives U.S. examples, colloquial in character, 1887–1908.

L 123: WG 157. *Either* of these *three* roads is good.   **LE**

        OD, 4 c, 1616–1845.

L 124: WG 159. You are older than *me*.   **LE**

        OD, 6 b, 1606–1804. Shakespeare, Richardson, Byron cited. *Hall EU*, 153, "It is found in Shakespeare, Swift, Prior, Pope, Southey, and A. H. Clough."

L 125: WG 178. What are the chances of *them* being found out?   **CE**

        Curme, *Syntax*, 489, "Often employed in colloquial speech." Cites Caxton and Latimer.

L 126: WG 116. There is *a* big *woods* behind the house.   **CE**

        OD does not record. *Webster*, "More often in pl. and often, chiefly in coll. use construed as a singular."

L 127: WG 127. I know it to be *he*.

    OD does not record he after the infinitive of the verb *to be*.

L 128: WG 95. Do you *wish* for some ice cream?   **LE**

    OD, vb. 2 a, 1526–1867.

L 129: WG 171. Intoxication is *when* the brain is affected by certain stimulants.

    OD and *Webster* do not record.

L 130: WG 154. *Neither* of your reasons *are* really valid.   **LE**

    OD, B 2 d, 1611–1875, citing Shakespeare, Dryden, Newman, and Ruskin.

L 131: WG 91. He *dove* off the pier.   **ALE**

    OD, 1882–1893, with comment, "U.S. and Eng. dial." *Webster*, "colloquial," but Horwill, *Modern American Usage*, 110, has twentieth-century literary examples. The *OD* citations are literary in character.

L 132: WG 142. Trollope's novels have already begun to *date*.   **LE**

    OD Sup, vb. 2, 1895–1928.

L 133: WG 141. Will you go? *Sure*.   **Dial**

    OD, adv. B 3 c, 1813–1862, "Dial."

L 134: WG 148. He is *kind of silly*, I think.   **CE**

    OD and *Sup.*, s.v. *kind*, sb. 14 d, 1796–1889, "colloq."

L 135: WG 117. I *will probably* come a little late.   **LE**

    OD, s.v. *will*, vb.[1] 16, 888–1923, with comment, "since 17th c. almost exclusively in Scottish, Irish, provincial, or extra-British use." While some citations are dialect, many are literary. *Jesp IV*, 256, "this usage is constantly gaining ground." Shelley and Shakespeare quoted. Curme, *Syntax*, 363, "In American colloquial speech *will* is now the

more common form in the first person." *"Shall . . .
is still the preferred form in the higher grades of the
literary language in America, though not so uniformly used as it once was."* Fries, "The Periphrastic
Future with *Shall* and *Will," Publications of the
Modern Language Association,* 40 (1925), 963 ff.,
"The first person with *will* has always predomi-
nated."

L 136: WG 145. That was the reason for *me leaving* school.   **CE**

Curme, *Syntax,* 489, "often employed
in colloquial speech." Latimer and Caxton cited.

L 138: WG 155. I'll swear that was *him.*   **CE**

OD, 3, 1605–1840, "Common in colloquial language from end of 16th century." Shakespeare, Johnson, and Burke cited.

L 139: WG 179. Well, that's *going some.*   **ACE**

OD, adv. C 2 c, 1866–1894, "U.S." The
examples, however, are colloquial in character.

L 140: WG 128. *Leave* me alone or else get out.   **LE**

OD, vb. 13, 1400–1885.

L 141: WG 161. Of two disputants, the *warmest* is
generally in the wrong.   **LE**

Curme PSA, 188, "Sometimes in the
literary language," cites Thoreau. *Jesp II,* 204,
"Found very frequently in good authors," with
range of illustrations 1470–1896, including Shakespeare, Defoe, Stevenson. See also *Hall EU,* 280,
and an article by Russell Thomas, "The Use of the
Superlative Degree for the Comparative," *English
Journal,* College Edition, 24 (1935), 821–829, where
over 75 examples of 23 adjectives from Literary
English, ranging in date from 950 to the present
time, are cited.

L 142: WG 182.   It was *good and cold* when I came
in.   ACE
  OD Sup, s.v. *good,* adv. B d, 1834–
1926, "U.S. Colloq."

L 143: WG 156.   We haven't *but* a few left.
  OD does not record.

L 144: WG 119.   In the collision with a Packard,
our car naturally got the *worse* of
it.   LE
  OD, sb. 4 b, 1205–1888; the citation
for 1860 is a phrase with *of.*

L 145: WG 143.   I wouldn't have said that if I had
thought it *would have* shocked
her.
  OD has no specific information on this
question of tense sequence.

L 146: WG 164.   *Yourself* and your guests are invited.   Dial
  OD (as simple subject) 4 a, 1400–
1799. *Webster,* "Archaic and dialect." *Hall EU,* 175–
176 cites 37 authors from Malory to Stevenson as
using the *self* forms but does not differentiate as to
the various possible uses.

L 147: WG 140.   The man was *very amused.*   LE
  OD, adv. B 2 c, 1641–1877.

L 148: WG 86.   Such *naif* actions seem to me absurd.   LE
  This spelling recorded in *OD* 1598–
1885.

L 149: WG 169.   It seems to be *them.*   CE
  OD, B 3 b, 1654–1888, "Common colloquially."

L 150: **WG** 166. Everybody bought *their* own
ticket.   **LE**
OD, 1530–1871, Sidney and Ruskin
cited.

L 151: **WG** 151. *Say,* do you know who that is?   **ACE**
OD, vb. 12 b, 1857–1888, "Colloq.
U.S."

L 152: **WG** 162. I suppose that's *him.*   **CE**
OD, 3, 1515–1840, Shakespeare and
Van Brugh cited. "Common in colloq. use from end
of 16th c."

L 153: **WG** 133. I *can't help but* eat it.   **LE**
OD, s.v. *help,* vb. 11 b, 1894.

L 155: **WG** 158. There is a row of beds with a curtain *between each bed.*   **LE**
Jesp II, 203, cites Shakespeare, Fielding,
and Dickens. *Curme,* although disapproving of the
construction, cites George Eliot.

L 156: **WG** 136. If I asked him he would *likely* refuse.   **ALE**
OD, adv. 13 2, 1380–1895, with com-
ment, "Rare exc. Scotch or dial." *Webster* records
without comment. Horwill, *Modern American Usage,*
190, has several examples of this construction.

L 157: **WG** 160. John didn't do so *bad* this time. **ACE**
OD Sup, 1816–1890, "U.S." The ex-
amples are chiefly colloquial in nature.

L 158: **WG** 92. Cities and villages are being
stripped of all they contain *not
only, but* often of their very inhabitants.
OD does not record.

L 159: **WG** 80. *Everybody's else* affairs are his
concern.   **LE**
Curme PSA, 170, "older form." *Hall*

EU, 87, cites instances of this construction in Thackeray, Mark Twain, and Henry James.

L 160: **WG 165. It *don't* make any difference what you think.**   ACE

OD Sup, s.v. *do,* A 2 c γ, 1670–1862, labeled "American." The examples are generally colloquial in character.

L 161: **WG 182. I read in the paper *where* a plane was lost.**   CE

OD, 10 c, citations range from 1300–1611 (two Shakespeare) and instances are given from modern colloquial speech.

L 162: **WG 146. That boy's mischievous behavior *aggravates* me.**   CE

OD, 7, 1611–1858, "familiar." Richardson and Thackeray cited.

L 165: **WG 129. Yes, our plan worked just *fine*.**   Dial

OD, adv. C 1 b, 1385–1890, "Dial."

L 166: **WG 153. The fire captain with his loyal men *were* cheered.**   LE

Curme, *Syntax,* 49, "The plural is often found here in older English and is sometimes still used." Cites *Bible,* I Tim. vi. 6. *Jesp II,* 176, cites Shakespeare, Bunyan, and Shaw.

L 168: **WG 137. The British look at this differently *than* we do.**   LE

OD, 1665–1844.

L 169: **WG 147. *Most* anybody can do that.**   ACE

OD and *Sup,* adv. B 4 b, 1770–1904, "Dial. and U.S." *Webster,* "Dial. and colloq."

L 170: **WG 149. It is *liable* to snow tonight.**   LE

OD, 3 b, 1682–1896. Horwill, *Modern American Usage,* considers it an Americanism, but the *OD* citations do not bear out his contention.

L 171: WG 168. They went in *search for* the missing child.

Not recorded.

L 173: WG 138. John *was raised* by his aunt.   **ALE**

OD, vb.[1] 10, 1744–1870, "Now chiefly U.S." Horwill, *Modern American Usage* cites examples from contemporary American writing.

L 174: WG 175. Martha *don't* sew as well as she used to.   **ACE**

See evidence for L 160 above.

L 175: WG 163. He *most* always does what his wife tells him.   **ACE**

OD and *Sup,* adv. B 4 a, 1584–1901, "Dial. and U.S." *Webster,* "Dial. and colloq."

L 177: WG 180. My experience on the farm helped me *some,* of course.   **ACE**

OD, adv. C 2 b, 1825–1889, "U.S." Horwill, *Modern American Usage* cites Lincoln Steffens. *Webster,* "colloq."

L 178: WG 152. It's *real* cold today.   **ALE**

OD, adv. B, 1658–1887, "Chiefly Sc. and U.S."

L 179: WG 172. His presence was valueless *not only,* but a hindrance as well.

Not recorded.

L 180: WG 174. We don't often see sunsets *like* they have in the tropics.   **LE**

OD, adv. B 6 a, 1530–1886, "Generally condemned as vulgar or slovenly though *examples may be found in many recent writers of standing.*"

L 182: WG 173. She leaped off *of* the moving car.   **Dial**

OD, adv. 7 b, 1593–1875, "Formerly and still dialectically." Shakespeare cited.

L 184: **WG** 170. It is only a little *ways* farther. ALE

OD, sb.¹ IV 23 c, 1588–1907. *Webster,* "Dial. and coll." Horwill, *Modern American Usage,* has examples from American writings.

L 185: **WG** 177. It looked *like* they meant business. ACE

OD and *Sup,* adv. B 6 e, 1493–1898, "Dial. and U.S." The U.S. examples are definitely colloquial.

L 187: **WG** 134. The child was weak *due to* improper feeding. ALE

OD and *Sup,* a 9, 1661–1886, "Freq. in U.S."

D. LINGUISTS, "DISPUTABLE"; WHOLE GROUP, "ILLITERATE."

L 137: **WG** 184. They *eat* [et] dinner at twelve o'clock. CE

OD, 1835, is latest citation for this spelling, although H. C. Wyld in his *Universal Dictionary* (London, 1931) considers *eat* the normal form and *ate* as obsolescent. OD, H. W. Fowler, *Modern English Usage,* and Daniel Jones, *An English Pronouncing Dictionary,* all of which record British rather than American pronunciation, give [et] as the more frequent form. Since this is a question of pronunciation rather than spelling, it is classed as a colloquial usage.

L 154: **WG** 185. *Aren't* I right? CE

Curme PSA, 248, gives twentieth-century examples and classes as colloquial.

L 163: **WG** 192. The stock market collapse left me *busted.* ACE

OD Sup, 1881–1920, "U.S. colloq."

L 164: **WG** 195. Neither author nor publisher *are* subject to censorship. LE

OD, A 1 d, 1759–1874. Johnson, Cowper, Southey, and Ruskin cited.

L 167: WG 198. Don't get *these* kind of gloves.   **CE**

   OD, sb. 14 b, 1564–1797, "common colloquially." Also *sort* with *these* or *those,* 1551–1872.

L 172: WG 191. I suppose I'm wrong, *ain't* I?   **CE**

   OD, latest citation, 1799, with comment: "Popular dialect of London and elsewhere." *Webster,* "dialect." *Curme PSA,* 248, classifies it as colloquial, and the illustrative citations are certainly not dialect.

L 176: WG 187. It *sure* was good to see Uncle Charles.   **ACE**

   OD and *Sup,* adv. B 3, 1425–1913, "Dialect, Irish, and U.S." Citations include Sidney, Milton, and Dryden.

L 181: WG 203. I am older than *him.*   **CE**

   OD, 3, 1759–1764, but the predicative *him* citations range from 1381–1840. "Common in colloquial language from the end of the sixteenth century."

L 183: WG 186. She *sung* very well.   **LE**

   OD citations up to 1877. *Webster* records without comment.

L 186: WG 190. Do it *like* he tells you.   **LE**

   OD, 1530–1886, "Now generally condemned as vulgar or slovenly, *though examples may be found in many recent writers of standing.*" Citations include Shakespeare, Southey, and William Morris.

E. LINGUISTS, "ILLITERATE"; WHOLE GROUP, "DISPUTABLE."

L 191: WG 181. The dessert was made with *whip* cream.

   Not recorded.

L 192: WG 180. Now just *where* are we *at?*   **ALE**

    OD Sup, s.v. *at,* prep. 1 d, 1859–1914,
"U.S."

L 193: WG 167. The kitten mews whenever it wants in.   **ACE**

    OD, s.v. *want,* vb. 4 f, 1844–1897,
"Scotch, North Irish, U.S. colloquial."

L 196: WG 176. *Reverend Jones* will preach.   **LE**

    OD, 2 c, last citation 1657, "In early use without *the.*" E. C. Ehrensperger in *American Speech,* October, 1931, 41, "In this country the practice of omitting *the* is widespread . . . the Boston *Transcript,* the *Harvard Alumni Bulletin,* many church periodicals, etc., omit it."

L 204: WG 139. The *data is* often inaccurate.   **ALE**

    OD, no information. *Webster,* "Not infrequently used as singular." Horwill, *Modern American Usage,* 96, cites Professors E. J. Haskin and C. McCarthy, and Col. House.

The results of this survey of the "disputable" expressions may be most conveniently presented in tabular form. The 121 items belonging to this group were found to be distributed among the various categories as shown on page 50.

Undoubtedly, the most striking feature of this tabulation is the high proportion of these expressions which are recorded as occurring in Standard English, written and spoken. Adding the fifty items which are recorded as belonging to Literary English, the thirteen to be found in American Literary usage, the twenty-five colloquial expressions and the eighteen American Colloquial, we find that 106 of the 121 items, which according to a survey of opinion seemed to be disputable, are, on the basis of recorded fact, actually in cultivated use today. This is a proportion of 87 per cent. Of the remaining fifteen items, six were in standard use at some previous time.

TABLE II

STATUS OF DISPUTABLE EXPRESSIONS IN RECORDED USAGE

C. E. U. Ranking	LE	ALE	CE	ACE	Dial	Arch	NR	Total
A. Linguists "established" Whole Gr. "disputable"	23	1	10	1	1	–	–	36
B. Linguists "disputable" Whole Gr. "established"	2	3	–	1	–	–	–	6
C. Both Gr. "disputable"	21	7	10	13	5	–	8	64
D. Linguists "disputable" Whole Gr. "illiterate"	3	–	5	2	–	–	–	10
E. Linguists "illiterate" Whole Gr. "disputable"	1	2	–	1	–	–	1	5
Total	50	13	25	18	6	0	9	121

LEGEND: *LE*—Literary English *Dial*—Dialect
 ALE—American Literary English *Arch*—Archaic
 CE—Colloquial English *NR*—Not Recorded
 ACE—American Colloquial English

We may conclude, then, first of all, that the teacher is not only safe in accepting the so-called "established" usages of the Leonard report, but there are seven chances out of eight that a "disputable" item is wholly current in standard English as well. Nor is there, from the evidence, any reason to suspect that these 106 items are to be considered particularly inelegant. In other words, the teacher may advise his pupils to avoid the "disputable" usages if he wishes to. That is his privilege. But his censure of these expressions cannot be on the basis that they are not to be found at present on the pages of reputable writers or in the mouths of cultivated speakers.

To the student of language this tabulation will demonstrate also how much more conservative a survey of opinion about language is apt to be than the facts of the language actually warrant. The *Introduction* to the grammar section of the Leonard report, maintained that dictionaries, because their citations were drawn from literary examples of acknowledged value, were necessarily slower and more conservative than usage itself, that the dictionary method, valid though it might be, must of necessity result in a lag of several years between the adoption of a given usage and its appearance in a dictionary.[17]

There are here two mistaken assumptions, one of which is expressly stated and the other implied. That the dictionary record of fact does not lag behind opinion, but on the contrary is well in advance of it, has been clearly demonstrated and needs no amplification. The implication that these disputable expressions are so new that they have not yet had time to be recorded in the dictionaries is likewise not borne out by the facts. Only nine of the 121 disputable expressions were not recorded in any of the sources used, and two of these nine (Nos. 158 and 179) are infelicities in style rather than matters of grammar. The *Oxford Dictionary* alone recorded all but twenty-three of the 121. Of the whole group of 121 disputable expressions, twenty-seven are recorded as arising in the nineteenth century, ten in the eighteenth, twenty in the seventeenth, twenty-two in the sixteenth, and twenty-four sometime before 1500; that is, either in the Middle or Old English periods. In other words, the expressions about which puristic objections center are not so much neologisms as they are old forms and usages of the language which are struggling to survive.

Finally, it is evident that this analysis should dispose once and for all of the journalistic cry of heresy and radicalism so frequently raised against the Leonard report. A survey of fact rather than of opinion would, in all probability, have increased the number of established usages from a meager seventy-one to 177.

---

[17] *Current English Usage*, p. 95. Reprinted in this monograph as page 65.

THE "ILLITERATE" USAGES

Before considering in detail the thirty-eight items which were voted "illiterate" by both groups of judges, it will be helpful to refresh our memory as to the implications of this term as it was used in the instructions to the judges. In the ballot, the fourth category was defined in the following terms:

4. Popular or illiterate speech, not used by persons who wish to pass as cultivated, save to represent uneducated speech, or to be jocose; here taken to include slang or argot, and dialect forms not admissible to the standard or cultivated area; usually called "vulgar English," but with no implication necessarily of the current meaning of vulgar: "naif, popular or uncultivated English."

It is unfortunate that when the results of the survey were put together the single word *illiterate* was chosen as a defining label to represent this whole group. In a country such as ours, where literacy is a virtual pre-requisite for respectability, the term *illiterate* serves to cast a gratuitous opprobrium upon any expression or group of expressions to which it is applied. Nor does it adequately sum up what is indicated by the detailed explanation quoted above. Certainly slang is not an "illiterate" form of expression; its use implies nothing about literacy, one way or another. Regional dialect forms may be used by speakers about whose cultivation there is no question. In terms of the definition given to the judges, "non-standard" would have been a much more accurate label. This term includes within its scope slang as well as regional and social dialects. None of these are Standard English. However the term "non-standard" says nothing more about these usages than just that, nor does it suggest anything about the social status, cultivation, taste, or literacy of those who use them.

Let us turn now to an examination of the factual sources for the evidence concerning those expressions which the judges considered beyond the pale of Standard English:

L 188: WG 199. John *had awoken* much earlier than usual.   **LE**

        OD, s.v. *awake* and *wake,* 1633–1924, but comments that *woken* seems obsolescent. *Curme PSA,* 306, cites Walpole and London *Times,* 1932, and comments, "In British English the strong forms *awoke, awoken,* woke, woken still occur in the past participle. In American English . . . confined to colloquial and popular speech." *Webster,* s.v. *awake* labels *awoken* "obs." but s.v. *wake* comments "sometimes *woken.*"

L 189: WG 209. I haven*'t hardly* any money.   **Arch**

        OD, 7, "Formerly sometimes (as still in vulgar use) with superfluous negative." One citation, 1674.

L 190: WG 196. The engine was hitting *good* this morning.   **Arch**

        OD, adv. B a, 13. .–1887, "Obs., rare except in vulgar or slang phrases."

L 194: WG 193. A woman *whom* I know was my friend spoke next.   **LE**

        OD, 11, 1467–1906, Dickens cited, but comments, "Used ungrammatically." *Jesp III,* 198, "The idiom is found in many authors of repute." Chaucer, Caxton, Shakespeare, Boswell, Shelley, Keats, Kingsley, Kipling, Galsworthy, Wells, Dreiser, and numerous others cited.

L 195: WG 206. He *drunk* too much ice water.   Arch

> *OD,* 1300–1648, *"drunk* began to reappear for sing. as well as pl. at end of 16th c. and is occasional to 19th." *Webster,* "formerly also *drunk."*

L 197: WG 207. All came except *she.*   Arch

> *OD,* 4, 1530–1881, "Now rare." Shakespeare cited three times.

L 198: WG 189. The *party* who wrote that was a scholar.   Arch

> *OD,* 14, 1541–1888, "Formerly common and in serious use; now shoppy, vulgar, or jocular." Jonson cited. *Webster,* "slang."

L 199: WG 197. My Uncle John, *he* told me a story.   Arch

> *OD,* 3, 1000–1839, all the citations except one are poetic. "Common in ballad style and now in illiterate speech."

L 200: WG 216. He *begun* to make excuses.   CE

> *OD,* 1563–1793, Pope cited. "An alternative from the old plural *begun* has also come down to the present day." *Curme PSA,* 307, marks it as an older literary form and comments that it survives in popular speech.

L 201: WG 200. I *calculate* to go soon.   ACE

> *OD* and *Sup,* 7, 1822–1859, "U.S. colloq." *Webster,* "Colloq. U.S."

L 202: WG 188. This is *all the further* I can read.   Arch

> Although *Current English Usage* says that this expression is not recorded in any dictionaries, *OD,* s.v. *all,* II 3 c, does give a group of constructions from which this undoubtedly arose. The citations range from 1250–1633.

L 203: WG 217. That *ain't* so.   Dial

> *OD,* 1778–1865, "Popular dialect of London and elsewhere." *Webster,* "Dial. or illit."

L 205: **WG 214.** He looked at me and *says* . . .   CE

> *OD*, vb.[1] 3 b ¶, 1682–1887, "In this use, the 3d sing. pres. is often substituted colloq. for the pa. t. *said*." *Jesp IV*, 19, "Very often this present tense (historic) alternates with the preterit." *Gammer Gurton's Needle*, Shakespeare (5 times), *Bible*, Defoe, Shaw cited. 1550–1903.

L 206: **WG 213.** I must go and *lay* down.   Dial

> *OD*, vb.[1] 43, 1300–1900, "Now (except in nautical language) it is only dialectical or an illiterate substitute for *lie*. . . . In the 17th and 18th centuries, it was not app. regarded as a solecism." Fielding and Byron cited.

L 207: **WG 210.** *Ain't* that just like a man.   Dial

> See evidence under L 203.

L 208: **WG 194.** Both leaves of the drawbridge *raise* at once.   ALE

> *OD*, vb.[1] 35, 1470–1761. *OD Sup* has later U.S. examples from reputable writers, 1770–1911.

L 209: **WG 202.** The people *which* were here have all gone.   Dial

> *OD*, 9, 1300–1703, "Now only dial. except in speaking of people in a body." *Webster*, "Arch. and dial."

L 210: **WG 204.** I *have drank* all my milk.   Arch

> *OD*, 1704–1819, "From 17th to 19th c. *drank* was intruded into the pa. pple., prob. to avoid the inebriate associations of *drunk*."

L 211: **WG 221.** *That there* rooster is a fighter.   Dial

> *OD*, 2 c, 1742–1863, "Dial. and vulgar." *Webster*, "Dial. and illiterate."

L 212: **WG 183.** The old poodle was *to no sense* agreeable.

> This item was generally misinterpreted by both compilers and judges. The vote was con-

sidered valueless at the time the Leonard report was written. See *Current English Usage,* 141, note 3 (p. 108 of the monograph). For this reason, it has been excluded from consideration here.

L 213: WG 205.   One of my brothers *were* helping me.

> *OD* and *Webster* do not record.

L 214: WG 201.   I enjoy wandering *among* a library.   LE

> *OD,* prep. A 2, 1175–1810, with collectives and mass words. The test sentence is from De Quincey. *Webster,* "Regularly followed by a plural or collective noun."

L 215: WG 211.   A light *complected* girl passed.   ACE

> *OD,* 1860–1873, "U.S. dial. or colloq." *OD Sup,* has further examples, 1822–1906. *Webster,* "Dial., U.S." Horwill, *Modern American Usage,* 78, "American colloquial."

L 216: WG 208.   I want *for you to come* at once.

> Not recorded in any of the sources.

L 217: WG 226.   He won't *leave* me come in.   ACE

> *OD Sup,* vb. 3 e, 1840–1910, "U.S. Colloq."

L 218: WG 228.   There was *a* orange in the dish.

> Not recorded.

L 219: WG 218.   It was dark when he *come* in.   Dial

> *OD,* 855–1888, "Hardly appears after 1500 in the literary language though still widely prevalent in Midland and Southern dialects." The *OD* treatment makes it difficult to separate the *come* spellings with phonetic values of [kom] and [kʌm].

L 220: WG 222.   You *was* mistaken about that, John.   Dial

> *OD,* s.v. *be,* vb. III 6.2 ¶, 1340–1837, "Still dial. in all persons." *Webster,* "Widely used

in the 18th century, often by standard authors, now regarded as grammatically incorrect or illiterate."

L 221: WG 229. I wish he *hadn't of* come. ACE

This involves two factors, the redundant use of *have, had,* in compound tenses and the unstressed *of* [əv] variant for *have.* Concerning the first, *OD* comments, s.v. *have,* vb. 26, "In 15th and 16 c. occur many instances of redundant *have, had,* in the compound tenses." Citations with *have* after *had,* 1470–1677, while *OD Sup* cites U.S. examples 1816–1911. Concerning *of* for *have, OD Sup,* s.v. *of,* comments, "U.S. dial. or coll. variant," and has citations 1847–1916.

L 222: WG 212. *Hadn't* you *ought* to ask your mother? CE

OD, s.v. *ought,* vb. IV 7 c, 1836–1895, "Mod. Dial." *Jesp IV,* 128, cites Bennett, Winston Churchill, Ade, and several examples from Sinclair Lewis. The examples in Jespersen appear to be colloquial rather than dialect.

L 223: WG 227. My cold *wa'nt* any better next day. Dial

OD, s.v. *be,* III 6 ¶, and s.v. *wa'n't,* 1702–1865, "Dialectically *were, war* (sg.) occur, hence the negative *warn't, wa'n't* in 18th c. dramatists." *Webster,* "Dial."

L 224: WG 223. If John *had of* come, I needn't have. ACE

See evidence for L 221.

L 225: WG 219. I had hardly *laid* down when the phone rang. Dial

See evidence for L 206.

L 226: WG 230. He did *noble*.

Not recorded.

L 227: **WG 224.** Somebody *run* past just as I
opened the door.   Dial

  OD, 1382–1869, "Dial." *Webster,*
"Dial."

L 228: **WG 225.** Just *set* down and rest awhile.   Dial

  OD, 5, 1205–1897, *set down,* s.v. *set,*
vb. 143 h (*b*), 1400–1809, "Dial. or vulgar." *Webster,* "Now illit. and dial."

L 229: **WG 220.** The neighbors took turns *setting*
up with him.   Dial

  See evidence for L 228.

L 230: **WG 215.** They *swang* their partners in the
reel.   LE

  OD, 1000–1912, "rarely *swang.*" *Curme
PSA,* 318, marks it as older literary form. *Webster,* "Archaic past tense."

  The results of this survey of the "illiterate" or non-standard expressions may be conveniently summarized in the following table:

TABLE III

Status of Illiterate Expressions in Recorded Usage

Literary English	4	Dialect	12
American Literary English	1	Archaic	8
Colloquial English	3	Not recorded	5
American Colloquial English	5		

  In interpreting the factual record of the "illiterate" expressions, we are faced with a situation somewhat different from that which prevailed with the disputable group. The "disputable" expressions, it will be recalled, were those concerning which a survey of opinion showed such divergence that a supplementary survey of fact was imperative if we were to come to any opinion about them. As to the thirty-eight items just examined, however, there was little or no lack of unanimity on the part of the judges.

All agreed fairly well in consigning them to the limbo of the illiterate. Because of this, the system of classification employed previously was left unchanged. That is to say, when an expression was labeled in the dictionaries as "dialect and illiterate," it was classified here as dialect; when it was labeled "illiterate" in present use but had obviously been in current use at an earlier period, it was classified here as "archaic." This procedure was followed in the hope that it might lead us to some useful conclusions about the nature of these non-standard expressions.

First of all, it should be noticed that thirteen of the thirty-eight items, roughly one-third, are recorded in reputable literary or colloquial use, either in England or America. Again the extreme conservatism of opinion about usage, as compared with the factual record of usage itself, is strikingly demonstrated.

It is also noteworthy that all but five of the thirty-eight items were recorded in the sources employed, and furthermore, that all thirty-three of those for which any record was found appeared in the *Oxford Dictionary* or its supplement. Thus we find that not only the disputable but even most of these condemned expressions were in accepted usage at some former period, but that over half of them (the twelve dialectal and the eight archaic) are now confined to particular regional or social dialects, that is to say, to limited, non-standard spheres of usage. We are reminded again how much of non-standard, "incorrect," or questionable language has a continuous history and tradition behind it; it is not created on the spur of the moment but, to indulge in a simile, is like an underground stream which pops up into the light of day where it is least expected and frequently not welcome.

There is one final observation to be made in connection with this group of expressions. This is in connection with the type of error or supposed error condemned as illiterate. According to the classification employed in the body of *Current English Usage,* the thirty-eight illiterate items represented sixteen different types of errors. Yet no less than twenty of the thirty-eight expressions were concentrated in those categories which dealt with the forms and uses of verbs. There were eight items which were concerned with past tense forms alone. Of the twenty expressions involving questions of verb form and use, seven were found to be Standard English, two archaic, and the remaining eleven were dialectal forms.

All of this would seem to suggest that in respect to matters of verb formation and use, our prejudices are heightened. This is particularly true of the past tenses of strong verbs. As a matter of fact, even the past tense form *sung,* given equal rank with *sang* by all of the factual sources, was rated as Literary English by two English teachers, as Colloquial English by fourteen, and as Illiterate by sixteen. This particular verb eventually ended up in the "disputable" category, but there is no overlooking the fact that 50 per cent of the judges considered a fully accepted verb form to be illiterate. The past participle *awoken,* still in literary use in England, was voted "illiterate," and it is particularly ironic that the very last item on the list, the most discredited, was the form *swang,* not at all uncommon in British speech.

VI

CONCLUSION

It is the earnest hope of both of the authors of this monograph that their attitude toward the Leonard study will not be misunderstood or misconstrued. There is no question in our minds as to the worth or significance of this pioneer work. We believe that it has accomplished much in the cause of linguistic liberalism. It has set forth an enlightened attitude toward language problems in a fashion that can be grasped by teacher and layman alike. It has undoubtedly influenced to a considerable extent the language textbooks which have been written and revised within the past few years. It is not, however, a final or definitive piece of work, and to consider it so would be a betrayal of the spirit in which it was conceived.

We trust as well that our attitude and procedure in the present study will not be misunderstood. We have considered it our function to supplement Leonard's work by displaying side by side with the opinions he collected, the record of usage of each item included in the original study. It has been our aim to be as objective as possible. The classifications of the various items are not to be taken as representing the opinions or the recommendations of the authors. We have endeavored to let the facts of the language speak for themselves, or at least those facts which appear in the most reliable and scholarly treatments of Modern English.

CURRENT USAGE IN GRAMMAR

REPRINTED FROM

CURRENT ENGLISH USAGE

By STERLING A. LEONARD

$\mathcal{S}$ I $\mathcal{Q}$

INTRODUCTION

The following brief statement of aims and methods is intended as an aid in the use and interpretation of the discussions and tables that follow.

Up to the present, almost the only authoritative statements of acceptable practice in English usage have had to be sought in dictionaries and handbooks. Dictionaries have as their prime function the recording of usage, but by their very nature most of their citations have to be drawn from literary examples of acknowledged value; this method, valid though it may be, must of necessity result in a lag of several years between the adoption of a given usage and its appearance in the dictionary. It has been shown that most handbooks are based on traditional pronouncements of dubious value,[1] but even where this is not the case, the value of the handbook is limited by the same consideration of time that handicaps the dictionary. Since—as the following study should make evident—allowable usage is based on the actual practice of cultivated people rather than on rules of syntax or logic, it seems desirable that some method be found whereby this practice can be ascertained and made available for reference. This study, it is hoped, constitutes at least a beginning of a research that, to be useful, should be constantly pursued in order that current usage may be placed on record.

The conclusions arrived at in the following pages were de-

[1] S. A. Leonard: *The Doctrine of Correctness in English Usage, 1700–1800.* University of Wisconsin Studies in Language and Literature, No. 25. Madison, 1929.

rived from a study of the results of two ballots. The first contained 102 expressions (indicated on Summary Sheet) of whose standing there might be some question. This ballot was submitted to a number of groups of judges whose standing qualified them to indicate what seemed to them to be the norm of usage among educated people generally. The first group of judges comprised a number of the foremost linguistic experts in the world—lexicographers, philologists, and grammarians. As trained observers of language ways, they were naturally qualified above all others to estimate the standing in actual cultivated use of the various items on the ballot. Therefore, in the following discussion of the separate items, their comments are given special prominence. Each item is followed by a number which indicates the rank assigned it by the votes of this group, though where the other groups show any significant divergence from the judgment of the linguists, the fact is noted. The second group consisted of active members of the National Council of Teachers of English. A third group was composed of well known authors; a fourth, of the editors of influential publications; a fifth, of leading business men; a sixth, of members of the Modern Language Association; and a seventh, of teachers of speech. Returns were received from 229 judges altogether. They should constitute a significant sampling of cultivated usage.

Following are the instructions to the judges as they appeared on the ballot:

The following list of expressions represents an attempt to present one or more examples from each of the levels or regions of usage suggested by Dr. Murray in the preface to the *New English Dictionary*. We hope by getting a consensus of expert opinion on the classification of these expressions to clarify and define more precisely the categories themselves. We shall be grateful if you will coöperate by placing in the blank to the left of each expression a number to correspond with one of the tentative definitions following. The word or phrase about which there is question of placement is underlined; no other part of the sentence which may perhaps belong to a different level should influence a judgment as to the crucial expression. The problem of pronunciation does not enter.

Score, please, according to your observation of what is actual usage rather than your opinion of what usage should be. For example, if you detest *like* as a conjunction, but observe it as a standard literary use, you should mark it *1*. Comments on any or all the expressions or on reasons for your placements will of course be most welcome.

Finally, please do not mark according to your own definitions of the categories or terms below—though we should be greatly helped if you cared to send in such definitions also; but for the purposes of this study use the definitions offered here, since all findings will have to be understood in the light of these:

Key Number   *Definitions of Terms*

1. Formally correct English, appropriate chiefly for serious and important occasions, whether in speech or writing; usually called "Literary English."
2. Fully acceptable English for informal conversation, correspondence, and all other writing of well-bred ease; not wholly appropriate for occasions of literary dignity: "standard, cultivated, colloquial English."
3. Commercial, foreign, scientific, or other technical uses, limited in area of comprehensibility; not used outside their particular area by cultivated speakers: "trade or technical English."
4. Popular or illiterate speech, not used by persons who wish to pass as cultivated, save to represent uneducated speech, or to be jocose; here taken to include slang or argot, and dialect forms not admissible to the standard or cultivated area; usually called "vulgar English," but with no implication necessarily of the current meaning of vulgar: "naif, popular, or uncultivated English."

In tabulating and evaluating the ratings on the ballots, marks of either 1 or 2 were taken as an indication that the expression in question is considered allowable for use by educated people, whether formally or colloquially. In certain instances, marks of 5 or higher expressed special reprobation. These were not numerous enough to make it worth while to give them special weights in the tabulations.

Ballot II consisted of 130 additional expressions of the same nature as those in Ballot I. This ballot, with the same instructions, was submitted to substantially the same list of judges in the groups of linguists and members of the National Council as received the first ballot. The other groups of judges were not asked to mark this ballot, and fewer judges in the groups named made returns—to be specific, returns were received from 17 linguists and 32 members of the Council. In view of the fact that these judges represented a highly selected group in so far as their qualifications were concerned, while they were quite unselected in regard to the shades of opinion they might have on matters of usage, their votes are probably significant in indicating the levels of usage to which the items on Ballot II at present belong. Because the judges marking Ballot II were fewer, perhaps the conclusions drawn from this ballot are slightly less reliable than those from Ballot I.

JUDGES' DISCUSSION OF SPECIFIC
ITEMS OF USAGE

The specific grammatical usages contained in the question-aries are grouped here for ready reference according to their grammatical classification, each item being accompanied by a general summary of the judges' estimate of its acceptability, and by any especially illuminating comment thereon.

Each item is followed by one of the following words as an indication of its probable usage status: *established, disputable, illiterate;* and by a number indicating its rank among the 230 usages, according to the linguists. The rank indicating most complete approval is one; that indicating most complete disapproval is 230. The ranking by the linguists is here given, as the expertness of this group of judges makes their opinion most significant. (For a list of the items arranged in the order of their acceptability, see pages 4–11.) Items marked *established* have been approved for literary or good colloquial use by at least 75 per cent of the judges and disapproved by not more than 25 per cent. *Disputable* items have been approved by fewer than 75 per cent and disapproved by more than 25 per cent. *Illiterate* items have been disapproved by more than 75 per cent of the judges and approved by fewer than 25 per cent.

The numbering of the headings in the following presentation has been so arranged that the arabic numerals always designate the specific examples of usage considered by the judges. The slight resulting inconsistency in the numbering scheme for certain sections is more than balanced by the greater ease in locating usage items.

Nouns

I. *Number*

1. There is a large *works* near the bridge. (29: established)

The English teachers ranked this much lower than did the linguists, placing it in the class of disputable usages. However, only 2 of 17 linguists disapproved it.

2. There is a big *woods* behind the house. (126: disputable)

British linguists remark that this expression is strange to them, though, as one says, "*a big works* is familiar."

In informal speech, this is probably acceptable in the United States.

3. The *data is* often inaccurate. (204: illiterate)

There was more disagreement among the various groups of judges on this item than on any other on either ballot. Possibly an additional jury of scientists would have added further to the confusion. Speech teachers (with only one judge among them disapproving), ranked this as 7 out of 100; business men ranked it 25, authors 38, and so on down to linguists, who ranked it 92. Uniformly with the other items, this expression is placed among illiterate usages on the basis of this last ranking; a composite judgment would have placed it high among disputable usages.

All that can be said definitely is that there is no dictionary justification for the singular use of this plural form, and that such use, from the point of view of cultivated usage, is still dubious, to say the least.

II. *Case*

1. *Pikes* Peak is in Colorado.[2] (105: established as technical)

Many of the judges were puzzled by this expression. One says: "I

---

[2] See also the conclusions as to this usage in the punctuation study, *Current English Usage*, p. 54.

don't understand what question arises here." Another asks: "Is *Pikes* here a misprint?"

This confusion possibly accounts for the relatively low rating of this expression by the judges, and especially by the linguists, who placed it lower than did any other group. Every other group yielded a majority for approval. The Standard Dictionary spells the name with the apostrophe; the New International spells it without.

Perhaps the two remarks (by linguists) which follow get at the root of the question:

"What was the trouble with this sentence? If it is the apostrophe, I should like to see that go. Has it not gone in many of the English names—Kings Warwick, and so on? That use of the possessive which ceases to be a possessive and sinks gracefully into the thing possessed —apparently a spiritual symbol of the devouring nature of all possessions!"

"A proper name of a place is determined by local usage."

There are, of course, many other instances of the suppression of an apostrophe in place names; for example, Teachers College, Citizens National Bank, etc. Both the spelling and pronunciation of place names properly follow local usage.

2. It is only a little *ways* farther. (184: disputable)

Judges and dictionaries agree, for the most part, that in spite of the historical justification for this form, it is now dialectal. The vote was about two to one for its inclusion among uncultivated usages.

PRONOUNS

I. *Classes*

a. INTENSIVE

1. They invited my friends and *myself*. (91: established)

One linguist says: "It occurs to me that I am willing to make an exception of Omar's 'Myself when young,' because of its sheer charm. But I would shut it out everywhere else save for emphasis."

The editors rated this highest, linguists second, business men last. 62 per cent of all the judges approved it, thus placing it low among established usages. This would suggest that, while perhaps people who are especially careful of their speech would avoid this expression, nevertheless it would hardly be safe to condemn it as incorrect.

2. *Yourself* and your guests are invited. (146: disputable)

This expression is approved by a majority of the linguists, disapproved by a large majority of the English teachers. It does not rank with the similar use of *myself*.

b. IMPERSONAL PERSONALS

1. *It* says in the book that . . . (62: established)

Although the English teachers rated this expression much lower than did the linguists, its right to be considered established in good colloquial usage is made quite clear by the linguists' large majority vote.

2. *You* had to have property to vote, in the eighteenth century. (76: established)

75 per cent of the judges approved this as good colloquial English; 12 per cent in addition aproved it as literary. The case for its inclusion among established usages is perfectly clear.

3. *They* had numerous strikes in England in 1860. (85: established)

This indefinite use of the pronoun they is approved as colloquial by five out of six of the judges.

c. RELATIVES

This is a man . . . I used to know. (Omitted relative) (9: established)

Only eleven of more than 200 judges condemned the omission of the relative by placing this expression in class 4. Nearly half of the judges approved this by placing it in class 1 (formal literary English); many of those approving it as colloquial English indicated that they believed it verged on literary English. It may be of interest to note that the editors placed this lower (rank 32) than did any other of the groups of judges, although even they accepted it as established.[3]

---

[3] See Jespersen's *Grammar*, Article on Hypotaxis.

Certainly no possible justification can be found for the practice some teachers still pursue, of requiring children always to insert the relative in such sentences.

II. *Gender*

1. Each person should of course bear *his or her* share of the expense. (11: established)

One linguist says: "I prefer simply *his*. This seems to be a matter of pleasing the women."
Another says: "Correct but not commendable."
This expression is correct but stilted. See note on item 1 under Articles in this chapter.

2. This is the chapter *whose* contents cause most discussion. (19: established)

None of the linguists, and only six (of 32) English teachers, condemned this as illiterate. The rest of the judges approved it. To insist that students use a phrase such as *of which* when speaking of inanimate objects is pedantic.

3. The people *which* were here have all gone. (209: illiterate)

"Which" is no longer in good standing when used to refer to people.

III. *Number*

1. *None* of them *are* here. (37: established)

Of the seven groups of judges, four are composed of teachers—linguists, English teachers, members of the M. L. A., and speech teachers; the other three are non-academic—authors, business men, and editors. It is worthy of note that the four groups of teachers placed this expression in the class of established usages, while the others considered it disputable. That is, 80 per cent of the former approved the expression, as against only 50 per cent of the latter. Among the authors the rank was 40; among the linguists, 12.

An editor, defending his estimate of the sentence as vulgar, says: " 'None of them are here' is not correct. It is perfectly correct to say 'None are here.' But 'None of them' must mean [sic] 'no one of them.' Hence it must be followed by the singular form of the verb."

The groups of teachers find justification for their estimate in those dictionaries which record usage. The N. E. D. says: "In later use *none* commonly with plural verb." (The earliest plural example recorded in this dictionary is of 1580.) The Standard says: "When the singular or plural equally well expresses the sense, the plural is commonly used." The New International testifies that "as subject, *none* with a plural verb is the common construction."

One linguist states: "The objection to *none are* never had any basis in good usage." An author says: "It is pure priggishness to pretend that *none* is always singular."

No authority can be found for condemning the use of "none" with plural verb. See also *kind . . . are* and *one . . . were*, in this same chapter under Verbs IV, items 1 and 3.

2. *Everyone* was here, but *they* all went home early. (98: established)

A business man remarks: "*Everyone* is synonymous with *all*, having a collective sense, and it seems to me quite permissible that the word *they* may follow."

The N. E. D. says: "The pronoun referring to *everyone* is often pl.; the absence of a sing. pronoun of common gender rendering this violation of grammatical concord sometimes necessary."

138 out of 200 judges approve this as colloquial usage; each group except that of the editors (where the votes are evenly divided) gives a majority for 1 or 2 (acceptable) as against 4 (uncultivated). Cf. *neither*, item 4 below.

3. *Everybody* bought *their* own ticket. (150: disputable)

Citations: Sam. Johnson: "Everyone sacrifices a Cow or more, according to their different degrees of Wealth or Devotion." Dasent (1870): "Everyone had made up their minds. . . ." Mallock, in *New Rep.* (1878): "Everyone then looked about them silently." Jane Austen uniformly employs this usage.

One speech teacher who marked this expression 2 says: "There is some justification for marking this 1." Another says: "Any pronoun here makes me uncomfortable."

A linguist comments: "The objection to *everybody . . . their* is largely theoretical. The best of writers have used it, and it fills a need."

A British linguist, in classing this as acceptable for cultivated colloquial English, says: "But *his* doesn't sound pedantic to me, and I think I say *his* myself."

Although a significantly large number of judges approved the expression, there is sufficient majority against it to indicate that it is not yet in good standing.

4. *Neither* of your reasons *are* really valid. (130: disputable)

A linguist says, "1 or 2—Older English, but still widely used by good authors."

The teachers ranked this lower than did the linguists; in both groups there was no decided disposition to place this definitely among illiterate usages.

5. *Neither* author nor publisher *are* subject to censorship. (164: disputable)

This sentence is from Galsworthy's *The Inn of Tranquillity*.

Linguists disagree about this expression. Two comments are: "Occurs in illiterate writing only. Loose colloq." "Not 1, but not 2 either, because it isn't colloquial enough."

The Standard Dictionary says: "Grammatical accuracy requires the use of a singular verb after the pronoun *neither;* this rule, however, is often disregarded in practice and infringements of it may be cited from good writers."

The Oxford Dictionary cites Johnson, Cowper, Southey, and Ruskin to show the use of *neither . . . nor* with two singular subjects and a plural verb. It is curious that, with so much evidence in favor of this usage from their most distinguished colleagues, the authors among the judges were almost unanimous in condemning the expressions as illiterate. In fact, every group of judges placed this lower than did the linguists.

Apparently this expression is losing ground, and is not in such good repute as once it was.

IV. *Reference*

1. I have no prejudices, and *that* is the cause of my unpopularity. (21: established)

25 per cent of the judges approved this as formal English; nearly all the rest approved it as colloquial.

2. **I went immediately into the banquet room, *which* was, I found later, a technical error. (47: established)**

In this instance the English teachers were less tolerant of the expression than were the linguists. Both groups, however, unite in approving this as established colloquial usage.

3. **"You just had a telephone call." "Did *they* leave any message?" (31: established)**

The great majority of judges approved this as cultivated colloquial English. See also section on impersonal personals.

4. ***One* rarely enjoys *one's* luncheon when *one* is tired. (4: established)**

Comments by linguists:
"*One* followed by one or more *one's* never wholly excluded *one* followed by one or more *he's*. A series of *one's* strikes many (including me) as a kind of pedantry. As a matter of fact, probably most people who stick rigidly to *one* have acquired it by effort."

"I rate this 1, but in effect it tends to 4, as semi-literate straining for correctness."

The comments and rating on this expression imply that, while correct, it is somewhat stilted.

5. ***One* rarely likes to do as *he* is told. (111: disputable)**

Comments:
"No such phrase used." (*Editor*)
"One is the proper form." (*Linguist*)
"Kruisinga points out that this construction is to be found in books; i. e.—'You know, my dear, if one esteemed such a person very much, and were quite sure, without any doubt, that he liked *you* in return . . .' (Meredith, *Evan Harrington,* Chap. 17). But generally speaking I should think it is to be discouraged." (*Linguist*)

"The English language's lack of a pronoun that satisfactorily combines he, she, and it, to my mind justifies the use of the masculine *he* in many cases where it is not quite correct." (*Business man*)

The frequent use of such a pronoun sequence as this is probably due to the desirability of avoiding such stilted locutions as that in item 4 (One rarely enjoys one's lunch when one is tired.). Every group of judges except the linguists regarded such usage as established. Probably it is quite correct, although perhaps the exceptionally careful speaker will by rephrasing avoid both stilted correctness and the looser construction illustrated here.

V. *Case*

1. It was *I* that broke the vase, father. (2 : established)

"Suggests the speaker who is so afraid of his English that he pushes 'correctness' beyond the limit. I so frequently hear 'for you and I,' etc., from speakers who have been over-corrected in the matter of 'it's me.' " (*Linguist*)

No judge disapproved this expression; all but 7 rated it 1.

2. It is *me*. (73 : established)

This is a construction which has been made the subject of newspaper editorials beyond counting; and every purist who has felt the sanctity of grammatical English threatened has gone forth to do battle against those who would permit the verb *to be* thus to be followed by an objective pronoun. The fact seems to be that schematic grammar has little to do with usage.

Many of the comments recorded were flatly contradictory. Here are some of them:

"Unpardonable grammar."

"Incorrect—*bad*—but used often by discriminating people who rebel against the formalism of 'it is I.' I prefer 'it is I.' "

"Many purists approve it, but it seems not to have gained respectability."

"This expression is used so commonly that, among certain classes of people, it is considered quite correct. Others, however, never use it."

"Emerging into 1 (literary English)."

"*I* sounds quite mad in certain cases; e. g., pointing to a photo: 'Which is I?' ! ! ! 'Oh, I see, that's I' ! ! ! Absolutely non-English, hang all the grammarians on earth."

This expression is listed here among the established usages on the basis of the way the linguists voted—only three of twenty-eight condemning it as illiterate. If all the judges' estimates had been taken into consideration, without weighting on the basis of the greater expertness of one group as against another, this sentence would have been placed among the disputable usages—only the business men, of whom eighteen condemned and five approved, would place it among expressions clearly illiterate. One hundred thirty judges altogether approved this; ninety-one condemned. This can hardly constitute sufficient reason for taking time to teach "it is I" in school. As a matter of fact, both forms are at present avoided by careful speakers. Further light on the importance of formal grammar as a guide to usage will be gained by considering the grammatically equivalent but not equally accepted expression *it is him.*

3. If it had been *us,* we would admit it. (102: established)

This is a borderline expression, approved by twenty-nine judges; condemned by nineteen. Certainly there is not enough evidence against it to make it possible to condemn it dogmatically as bad English, with such a majority in its favor, although it is not on a par with "It is me."

4. I'll swear that was *him.* (138: disputable)

This also falls among the list of usages that are disputable, but not unquestionably wrong.

5. I suppose that's *him.* (152: disputable)

One linguist says: "Probably less firmly established than *that's me.*"

Another remarks: "I am rather uncertain about the pronoun after *to be.* 'It's me' I use and consider correct. 'It's us' I have misgivings about, but I think I have used it or would use it. 'It's him' I like least of all."

It seems safe to say that grammar has little, if anything, to do with the validity of such constructions as this. A review of the judgments on other similar expressions (see items 1, 2, 3, 4 in this section) will show clearly that "correctness," in such cases at least, is entirely a matter of usage, and has little to do with logic and less with grammar.

This particular expression, while approved as educated colloquial usage by a significant number of judges, has not won the approval accorded the objective form of "me" or even "us" after forms of "to be."

6. You are older than *me*. (124: disputable)

The English teachers rated this lower than did the linguists. Of the latter, two-thirds approve the expression as good colloquial English.

7. I am older than *him*. (181: disputable)

Linguists say:

"Personally I generally say 'I am older than *he is.*' But never 'older than *he.*' Sometimes, no doubt, 'older than him.'"

"We all know that these expressions are taboo. Also that most people (educated or otherwise) use them to the exclusion of the alternate form."

"4, possibly merging into 2."

Speech teachers and business men place this expression at the bottom of the list of expressions on the first ballot; the other groups of judges place it higher, but there is a decided majority against its inclusion among allowable expressions.

8. A woman *whom* I know was my friend spoke next. (194: illiterate)

The judges' rating places this expression definitely among uncultivated usages. Cf. Jespersen: *Philosophy of Grammar*, Appendix A.

9. I took it to be *they*. (116: disputable)

A linguist says: "I consider *them* the 'correct' form, but I fancy people use *they* a good deal. I don't consider this form as bad as 'for she and I,' etc."

The linguists rated this expression considerably higher than did the English teachers, a large majority of whom condemned it as illiterate. It cannot be considered either as established or as definitely uncultivated.

10. I know it to be *he*. (127: disputable)

A linguist says: "This strikes me as a concocted phrase that would hardly be used. People say either 'I know it's *he* (or *him*).' "

A small majority of the judges consider this expression as uncultivated.

11. It seems to be *them*. (149: disputable)

An author says: "Stevenson and others use this but it jars me."

A British linguist says: "I don't think I should ever say 'It seems to be *they*.' " Another comments: "Probably 'it seems to be them' and 'it is them' are not quite in so good use as 'it is me.' "

A majority of the judges condemn this expression as uncultivated, although 35 per cent approve it as good colloquial usage. It is obvious that this expression has not the same standing as "it is me," which seems to demonstrate that formal grammar has little to do with correctness in matters of this sort.

12. Invite *whoever* you like to the party. (81: established)

A linguist remarks: "The indefinite *who(ever)* seems to follow the same law as the interrogative."

The linguists rated this expression higher than did the English teachers, only two out of sixteen condemning it. Thirty-three of the forty-eight judges approved this use of the nominative case as acceptable colloquially.

13. *Who* are you looking for? (74: established)

The linguists rated this higher than did any of the other groups of judges; the other groups placed the expression among disputed usages. All the groups except the business men and authors gave majorities for approval.

N. E. D.: "Common in colloquial use as object of a verb or preposition following at the end of a clause."

Comments by linguists:

"In our best literature this construction has been waning for centuries. *Whom* is now the literary form."

"Many grammarians fail to note that only the interrogative, not the relative *who* is in good colloquial use as objective case."

" 'Whom are you looking for' non-English. 'For whom are you looking' possible book English, but only with some prepositions; viz., when the preposition is not felt to make, with the verb, a compound. I couldn't say or write 'without whom can we do?' I should write, as I should say, 'Who can we do without?' I should write, too, 'Who are you looking for?' etc., like Shakespeare."

Apparently this is acceptable in informal spoken English, but most authorities do not approve it for written English.

14. All came except *she*. (197: illiterate)

A linguist says: "There is a historical basis for the nominative with both *but* and *except,* though for different reasons. Cf. Chaucer, Cl. T. 508. But probably present-day use is based on an effort to be 'correct.' "

Of fifteen linguists, two considered this expression allowable; the English teachers were unanimous in condemning it.

15. *Everybody's else* affairs are his concern. (159: disputable)

Comments by linguists:
"Artificial."
"Pedantic."
"Nowhere used." (British)

"Not English—pseudo-correction by the semi-literate for *everybody else's,* which is good colloquial English."

"Curme has here pointed out the true syntactical principle that has led the popular instinct: the genitive sign immediately precedes the governing noun."

It is significant that English teachers, possibly influenced by the pronouncements of sundry handbooks, would place this among established usages. Over half the linguists, on the other hand, consider the expression as illiterate or semi-literate. There can be no question, at any rate, that "everybody else's" is infinitely to be preferred. See note on Articles, item 1, in this chapter.

VI. *Most as an Adjective*

Most anybody can do that. (169: disputable)

All the dictionaries and most of the linguists agree in classifying this expression as dialectal, although one expert cites a sentence from *Harper's Magazine* beginning "Most anyone at the Peace Conference . . ."

The judges were about equally divided between approval and condemnation of this expression.

VII. *Much as a Pronoun*

This much is certain. (25: established)

This expression was unanimously approved, the majority of judges rating it as cultivated colloquial English.

VERBS

I. *Classes: Transitive and Intransitive Confused*

1. I must go and *lay* down. (206: illiterate)

One linguist remarks that, while this expression is not now sanctioned by usage, it was "good in the 18th century."

There was little disagreement among the judges on this expression, over 93 per cent of them disapproving it.

2. I had hardly *laid* down again when the phone rang. (225: illiterate)

This expression was nearly unanimously condemned as vulgar.

3. The sailors *laid* out along the yards. (106: established as technical)

As this is recorded in the dictionaries as a technical nautical term, it might have been so listed; but it was so ordered by only one out of five judges. Most of the remaining 80 per cent condemned the expression, in spite of such dictionary authority as: "*Lay*, v.i. . . . 2. Naut. to place oneself in a certain position." (Standard Dictionary.)

4. Just *set* down and rest awhile. (228: illiterate)

Set, used intransitively in this way, is an undoubted solecism in present usage.

5. The neighbors took turns *setting* up with him. (229: illiterate)

A solecism.

II. *Tense*

A. CONFUSION AMONG FORMS OF

a. FUTURE: *shall* AND *will*

1. My colleagues and I *shall* be glad to help you. (46: established)

One linguist says of this expression that it is "not illiterate but pedantic." A British linguist says the expression is "not used."

There is a curious disagreement on this expression between the English teachers and the linguists. Of the teachers, none disapprove, and 75 per cent consider it appropriate to the most formal uses. Of the sixteen linguists, four disapproved altogether, while the remaining twelve were evenly divided between approval as formal literary English and as good colloquial usage.

Such disagreement among experts, while exhibiting a strong tendency towards complete approval, gives little justification for dogmatism on the subject of "shall" and "will" by teachers.

2. I *will probably* come a little late. (135: disputable)

N. E. D.: "In the first person, *shall* has, from the early Middle English period, been the normal auxiliary for expressing mere futurity."

Comments by linguists:

"Soon will be acceptable as literary."

"Creeping into current use—disliked by elder people. It was considered a Scotticism."

"This is still 'popular illiterate' speech to me, but I believe that a generation or two will see the distinction lost."

"Personally, I should say *shall,* here. But I fancy I am one of a minority, and I am quite familiar with *will.*"

"I find few who use *shall* according to correct rules."

"Good. *Will,* I take to refer to one's own volitions; *shall* to outside influences."

These comments show how unwilling experts are to dogmatize on the distinction (if any) between *shall* and *will.* The whole matter is at present surrounded by a cloud of uncertainty. The only thing about which there seems to be no doubt is that the hard and fast rules laid down by most rhetorics and handbooks are not to be relied on; probably what distinction ever has existed is gradually disappearing. About two-thirds of the judges approved this particular sentence.

3. I'd *like* to make a correction. (53: established)

A linguist remarks: "*I would like* is a well established idiom with those particular about the distinction between *shall* and *will.* I have suspected that the old construction *me would like* had something to do with this. I do not agree that there is no historical basis for the modern distinction, though probably there were different lines of development in different dialects."

Only one of forty-seven judges condemned the expression as illiterate; nearly all the rest approved it as colloquial.

4. *Will* you be at the Browns' this evening? (58: established)

A linguist says: "2 (cultivated colloquial English) if inviting. More doubtful if questioning—though *shall you* sounds affected to me (not pedantic, just affected, tony)."

This is generally approved as colloquial English. In fact, nearly a quarter of the judges considered it appropriate for formal use.

b. PAST

1. He *begun* to make excuses. (200: illiterate)

The Standard Dictionary says, "*Begin; began* or *begun.*"

The N. E. D. says: "*Began,* established as the standard form; the alternative *begun* has also come down to the present day."

Only 5 per cent of the judges (all from among the linguists, English teachers, and members of the M. L. A.) approve this form even for colloquial English; it is condemned as illiterate by the remainder.

2. He *drunk* too much ice water. (195: illiterate)

Dictionaries all record the fact that this form was once correct; the N. E. D., for instance, says, "Occasional to 19th century."

Linguists and members of the Modern Language Association, probably because of their awareness of the historical justification for this form, place it higher than do the other groups of judges, although even they disapprove it by large majorities. Evidently it has almost altogether lost the standing it once had.

3. Somebody *run* past just as I opened the door. (227: illiterate)

The condemnation of this expression was nearly unanimous.

4. She *sung* very well. (183: disputable)

Comments by linguists:

"I didn't feel able to characterize *sung*, etc. I don't use them myself and they *seem* to me rather like vulgarisms, but they are historically as good as *sang*, etc., they have plenty of good recent literary currency, and they may occur colloquially to a greater extent than I have ever noticed."

"With the best intentions, I find that my numbering is not consistent. The preterite *drunk* I have seen so often that I put it under 2, but *sung* and *begun* I have consigned to 4—where, by my own feeling, all three of them belong."

"The past tense *sung* seems to me perhaps slightly better than *begun* and *drunk*, but it is probably used now—except in poetry—only by old-fashioned people."

The New International, Standard, and Oxford Dictionaries give both *sang* and *sung* as preterite; the later adds: "Recent usage . . . has mainly been in favor of *sang*."

With the exception of the English teachers, who rank this expression as nearly established, the judges place this rather low on the list. Once correct, it seems to be going out of fashion in favor of "sang."

5. They *swang* their partners in the reel. (230: illiterate)

All but one of the judges (all the linguists) rated this expression as illiterate. See also items 1, 2, 3, 4 in this section.

6. It was dark when he *come* in. (209: illiterate)

This expression was rated illiterate by a practically unanimous vote.

7. He *dove* off the pier. (131: disputable)

The dictionaries characterize *dove* as colloquial; the N. E. D. adds that it is "U. S. and Eng. dial."

A linguist says: "Good colloquially; perhaps acceptable as literary."

Another says: "*Dove* seems to be regularly used even in good writing. I fancy *dived* seems archaic and biblical to most people."

There was more disagreement among the judges about this than about most expressions. The general trend, however, seems to be toward its acceptance, though it is not yet fully admitted to the category of accepted written usages.

8. They *eat* [et] dinner at twelve o'clock. (137: disputable)

Standard Dictionary: "*ate* or *eat* (*ate* is now preferred by many as the past tense of *eat,* but the usage is debatable)."

New Int. Dictionary: "pret. *eat, ate* (in Eng., commonly *et*)."

N. E. D.: "The pronunciation *et* is commonly associated with the written form *ate,* but perhaps belongs rather to *eat,* with shortened vowel after analogy of weak verbs *read, lead,* etc."

Comments:

"Would not use this myself." (Canadian linguist)

"I always say i:t, et, i:tn, never eit." (British linguist)

"This is good British English." (British linguist)

"The preterit of *to eat* is pronounced *et* in England, but I am aware that this is vulgar in America. It is generally spelt *ate,* but I have an idea it may be spelt *eat* thus falling into the category of *read,* rid, *read,* red. But perhaps your point is whether it is befitting to use the verb *to eat* and the names of meals as the direct object. Educated usage is, I think, *to have* dinner, etc." (British linguist)

"This English form is despised in the Southern U. S." (Speech teacher)

"Good English, bad American." (Author)

This expression is clearly entirely correct in England, incorrect in the United States.

9. He looked at me and *says* . . . (205: illiterate)

96 per cent of all the judges regarded this as uncultivated or illiterate.

c. PERFECT

1. John *had awoken* much earlier than usual. (188: illiterate)

Comments by linguists:

"Sounds grotesque in U. S. Correct in England."

"Older English, now receding."

For the United States, at any rate, this expression is not in good repute.

2. I *have drank* all my milk. (210: illiterate)

"Good English in the 17th and 18th centuries," says a linguist; "the present use is, I think, not a survival, but a sophistication." This expression is not now approved by educated people. See *drunk, sung, begun* in section on "Confusion as to Forms of Past Tense."

3. They have *gotten* a new car this year. (113: disputable)

Both linguists and dictionaries testify that this form is acceptable in the United States, although it is nearly obsolete in England. One linguist remarks: "The participle form *gotten* is the usual form in older English, and naturally the Pilgrim Fathers brought it with them to New England. It is the usual form in the colonial days and still the usual American form except in its function as auxiliary, where it is naturally replaced by *got*. I have collected a convincing list of examples of *gotten* from our best writers. There is no doubt that *gotten* is established in this country. In England it has almost disappeared."

4. My contention has been *proven* many times. (109: disputable)

Both dictionaries and judges differ widely on the propriety of *proven* as an acceptable variant of *proved*. The Standard calls it "archaic"; the New International lists it as a variant of *proved;* the N. E. D. says that it is "used properly in passive."

The linguists, authors, and editors place it among the disputable usages; the other groups of judges regard it as established. One linguist says: "Would not use this myself." Another: "The sound of *proven* possibly helps to explain its use over *proved*." A British linguist calls it "affected"; a southern linguist remarks that *proven* is "general in Arkansas."

It is hardly possible, in view of this uncertainty, to classify the word authoritatively, except to say that it cannot be regarded as illiterate, though "proved" seems to be generally preferred.

B. Sequence of

1. Galileo discovered that the earth *moved*. (12: established)

One judge says: "This attraction is too common to be condemned." This expression was rated 2 (cultivated colloquial) by a majority of the judges. One-third of the judges, however, rated this 1. It is evidently perfectly correct.

2. I wouldn't have said that if I had thought it *would have* shocked her. (145: disputable)

The judges were almost evenly divided between approval and condemnation of this expression. It seems to belong in that class of expressions which are careless but not absolutely incorrect.

III. *Moods: the Subjunctive*

1. If it *wasn't* for football, school life would be dull. (63: established)

A great majority of the judges approve this use of the indicative as good colloquial usage.

2. **I wish I *was* wonderful. (From Barrie's *Dear Brutus*)
(93: established)**

It is probable that less than fifty years ago the judgment upon this expression would have been quite different; the decay of the English inflected subjunctive is vividly illustrated by the fact that two-thirds of the judges approved this as good informal English.

IV. *Agreement with Subject*

1. **The kind of apples you mean *are* large and sour. (77: established)**

Only one from among sixteen linguists condemned this as illiterate; the rest considered it colloquially correct. The English teachers concurred, in general.

2. **The fire captain with his loyal men *were* cheered. (166: disputable)**

Comments by linguists:
"There is good literary authority for classing this as 2."
"Not 1, but not 2 either, because it isn't colloquial enough."
"Here *with* is equivalent to *and,* or analogous semasiology."
This expression is certainly ungrammatical, yet in informal conversation would probably be used by educated people. It would probably fall under the classification of 2.

There were few expressions on which so much disagreement was manifested among the judges; out of a hundred expressions, this was ranked all the way from 34 down to 82. A significant number (13) of judges (but no linguists) classified this as good literary English, but there was a small majority in favor of classifying it as uncultivated, not, however, enough to establish it as such.

3. **One of my brothers *were* helping me. (213: illiterate)**

This expression was very definitely rated as illiterate.

4. **There *was* a bed, a dresser, and two chairs in the room. (90: established)**

It is noteworthy that the speech teachers ranked this higher than did any other group of judges. Business men and editors ranked it lowest. Authors, in most cases the most severe group of judges, ranked this relatively high.

A linguist writes: "In good use from early times (OE). An interesting sample is: William Vaughn Moody, *Milton's Complete Poetical Works*, p. 32: I heard Israel Gollancz say, 'There was the Chief Justice and many distinguished men . . .' "

This expression cannot be considered wrong in informal cultivated English speech.

5. It *don't* make any difference what you think. (160: disputable)

This expression is still to be avoided, but it cannot definitely be placed among the illiterate usages, in face of its approval by nearly 40 per cent of the judges.

6. Martha *don't* sew as well as she used to. (174: disputable)

Over one-third of the linguists approved this as colloquial English; the proportion of English teachers approving it was a little lower. "Doesn't" is apparently, by a widening majority, the approved locution.

7. *Aren't* (*'nt* or *rnt*) I right? (154: disputable)

An American linguist says: "The English seem to have succeeded in putting over *aren't I*. I still do not care for it."

Comments by British linguists:

"Kittenish."

"British colloquial, coming into use in the U. S."

"I *say* this in familiar speech. I shouldn't write it. I fancy the majority avoid it."

"Acceptable as colloquial usage—also *ain't!*"

"*Ant,* no apostrophe (a :nt). I should spell (a :nt) *ant* without apostrophe (unless I were writing to a purist, in which case I should spell it *aren't*)."

The linguists rated this expression considerably higher than did any of the other groups of judges. This is perhaps influenced by the number of Britons among the linguists. The expression is evidently good colloquial usage in England, but has not yet found acceptance in the United States.

8. You *was* mistaken about that, John. (220: illiterate)

It is of interest that none of the expressions on Ballot I received a unanimous vote of all the judges, either for approval or disapproval. This expression and "wa'nt" were the only ones that no linguist approved.

A linguist says: "Good 100 years ago."

An author remarks: "In Fielding and others of his time *you was* was used of one person; *you were* of more than one."

Those who appeal to historical considerations for the defense or rejection of any expression must be given pause by the fact that this form, approved by only one per cent of the judges, has an immaculate historical justification.

V. *The Infinitive*

a. SPLITTING

1. The invalid was able *partially to raise* his body. (5: established)

Linguists say: "This is pedantic"; "I usually split the infinitive in colloquial speech"; ". . . But not commendable."

Correct but stilted.

2. We can expect the commission *to at least protect* our interests. (55: established)

Business men and English teachers ranked this higher than did the linguists; authors and speech teachers, who alone considered it disputable usage, ranked it lowest.

One speech teacher, without classifying the sentence, questions it as ambiguous. Another says: "Not a question of usage but of coherence."

A business man says: "I have little sympathy with the objection to the split infinitive. As a matter of fact, I believe a split infinitive with a word modifying the verb frequently adds strength as well as clarity to the sentence."

Comments by various linguists:

"This still connotes illiteracy to me, but I think it is only because one of my old professors taught me to slander it."

"Many writers split infinitives at will, and defend the practice."

"The particular sentence is awkward—but a split infinitive is O. K., as such."

"In this particular phrase the split infinitive seems to me rather unhappy. Sometimes it is perfectly legitimate and even necessary."

"I do not like the cleft infinitive but it is infinitely used."

"The use of the split infinitive is *in fact* sufficiently common in good writing to class it in 1. Common sense suggests its avoidance when nothing is gained in clearness."

" 'So as to always fit' (Dean Swift). Swift's occasional splits are not a conclusive argument. But the thing to note is that Swift, following his instinct for style, saw that it was better to split 'to fit' than to split 'so as to.' Not so your purists. They will give you 'owing, however, to' because no rule of thumb forbids. So they see no objection to 'used often to go' which to me is non-English, whereas 'used to often go' only offends against the rules of the porridge-brained (i. e., grammarians) and *is* English. Further, the purists never even notice the split in 'he did it even though he oughtn't to' —(they used to, but now they don't)—nor in 'to come and go.' "

The evidence in favor of the judiciously split infinitive is sufficiently clear to make it obvious that teachers who condemn it arbitrarily are wasting their time and that of their pupils.

b. DEBATED PHRASES

1. We will *try and get* it. (49: established)

Except for the speech teachers, a majority of whom condemned this expression, the judges for the most part approved this as appropriate for cultivated colloquial English—10 per cent of them considered it as belonging to literary English. Milton employs it. All dictionaries sanction it as colloquial.

A British linguist says: "*Try and* but not *tried and, tries and,* etc. Only the form *try*—e. g., *will try and*—an important observation purists miss of course."

This expression is evidently perfectly correct for cultivated colloquial use.

2. I want *for you to come* at once. (216: illiterate)

Nineteen out of twenty judges in all groups rated this expression as illiterate. It is, however, in cultivated use in the South of the

United States. This would seem to indicate that, in the estimation of the judges, dialect usages are generally equivalent to illiterate.

3. The kitten mews whenever it *wants in*. (193: illiterate)

Linguists and dictionaries agree that this expression is dialectal in certain localities—chiefly Scotland and here and there in the United States. In those localities where it is current, it may be allowable as a popular colloquialism; it has no standing for more formal or general use.

VI. *Participles, Debatable Uses of*

1. I will go, *providing* you keep away. (86: established)

Although 135 judges approve this, as against 83 who disapprove, all the groups except the linguists place it among the disputable usages.

A British linguist remarks: "To me this sounds vulgar but is gaining ground in newspapers (which generally, I may mention, set a pretty high standard in England) and is given in Concise Oxford Dict. (vide *provide*, ad. fin. 'providing that'—foll.). The following word is *provided;* the Conc. Oxf. seems therefore to suggest that *provided* is preferable, though it does not, as I should, condemn *providing.*"

The N. E. D. says: "providing, present participle. Quasi-conjunction (without *that*). On condition that; in case that; if only."

With so decided a majority in its favor, and with such dictionary evidence to support it, it would be hard to justify any campaign to eliminate this expression from the vocabulary of school children.

2. The child was weak, *due to* improper feeding. (187: disputable)

The linguists and the members of the Modern Language Association voted about two to one against the inclusion of this expression among the approved usages; the other groups of judges gave a considerable majority in its favor. There was wide disagreement among the groups as to the proper placement of the expression; it must be included, therefore, among the disputed usages.

Linguists remark:

"Good colloquial English in the sense used."

"I dislike this, but it is certainly in wide use."

"Used by all military writers."

"This would be unobjectionable in England, but I imagine that in America it would sound much as 'I guess' does to us. I think the American usage is better."

"*Due to* is particularly annoying to me; but it is rapidly gaining headway."

The N. E. D. lists this expression as "rare before the 19th century."

VII. *Gerund, Possessive with*

1. **What was the reason for *Bennett making* that disturbance? (95: established)**

A linguist says: "This is difficult to classify because it is considered good usage in British English, but the possessive seems to be used with proper names in American English." [Perhaps for reasons of euphony.]

Another linguist comments at some length: " 'For me making' sounds wrong, and yet not vulgar. A kind of careless colloquialism, rather than a solecism. 'For it making' sounds correct, but I think I say 'for its making.' With nouns I fancy I say 'through the dog making such a noise' as often as 'dog's.' I would never correct a child for saying 'dog,' especially as it is more logical. It is not the *making* which happened to be the dog's that's in question, but the *dog-making* fact. *Making* cannot be mistaken for a participle, because in that sense we should say 'which was making.' Even if it were mistaken for a participle, it is a less evil than the other word (not *word's* please) being mistaken for a plural. Moreover, 'dog making' allows an important distinction:

(1) 'I was surprised at Bennett bowling' (that he bowled).

(2) 'I was surprised at Bennett's bowling' (that it was so good or bad)."

Each group of judges except the authors gives a decided majority for approval of this expression as good colloquial English.

2. What are the chances of *them* being found out? (125: disputable)

Comments, by linguists:

"Illiterate, but some seemingly parallel cases are not objectionable."

"Not the best use, but defensible."

"Personally, I should use the full gerund (*their being*) here. But this construction doesn't shock me, and is, I think, very common."

This expression can hardly be considered apart from the one above. ("What was the reason for *Bennett making* that disturbance?") It is interesting to note that in the latter instance the linguists ranked the expression lower than did the other groups of judges, although they approved it by a large majority; whereas the linguists ranked the expression now under consideration much higher (17 for, 10 against) than did any of the other groups. Sentences 1, 2 and 3 in this section are grammatically similar; yet 2 and 3 are decidedly less approved than 1.

Apparently the possessive of a proper name before a gerund is less obligatory than that of a pronoun. The above pronoun form, while passable for the most informal English, is to be avoided.

3. That was the reason for *me leaving* school. (136: disputable)

A linguist says that this is entirely correct, "but not commendable."

Opinion is nearly evenly divided as to the standing of this expression. In the present state of usage, it cannot definitely be said to be either decidedly right or wholly wrong.

VIII. *Faulty Verb Forms*

1. I suppose I'm wrong, *ain't* I? (172: disputable)

A British linguist says: "Good colloquial English, but old fashioned."

Six of seventeen linguists considered this expression appropriate to the colloquial uses of educated people; the English teachers were nearly unanimous in condemning it. It stands very near the line established in this study between the disputable and the entirely disreputable usages. See also *aren't I,* etc.

2. *Ain't* that just like a man? (207: illiterate)

There is clearly a distinction in usage between this expression and *ain't* with the first person singular, where a commonly accepted interrogative contraction is lacking. As used here, "ain't" is almost unanimously condemned.

3. That *ain't* so. (203: illiterate)

Nearly all the judges condemned this form.

4. My cold *wa'nt* any better next day. (223: illiterate)

A British linguist says: "Purely American to me."
An American linguist remarks: "This is used by some northern New Yorkers, as I have heard; I have heard it used by a few in North Carolina; I think it is decidedly illiterate."
Only two among over 200 judges approved this for colloquial use. Decidedly it is not justified for use by educated people.

5. The stock market collapse left me *busted*. (163: disputable)

Some support for this expression as colloquial English may be found among the linguists; the English teachers are almost unanimous in condemnation.

6. The dessert was made with *whip* cream. (191: illiterate)

75 per cent of all the judges rated this expression as illiterate.

IX. *Nouns Made Into Verbs*

1. We *taxied* to the station to catch the train. (65: established)

The linguists were unanimous, and the English teachers nearly so, in classifying this as cultivated colloquial English.

2. He stopped to *price* some flowers. (70: established)

Two-thirds of all the judges regard this expression as acceptable colloquial English.

3. He *loaned* me his skates. (99: established)

The British linguists remark that the verb "loan" is not used in England. Forty-one of the forty-seven judges, however, approve the expression as acceptable.

4. The banker *loaned* me $200 at 6%. (104: established as technical)

195 of the 229 judges approved this use of *loan;* a quarter of these considered it acceptable as formal or literary English. Fifty-four judges classified it as technical. Their view is supported by the dictionaries (so long as the term is used in connection with finance); the dictionaries point out, however, that the use of *loan* as a verb as a verb is restricted chiefly to the United States.

The distinction between "loan" and "lend" among bankers and business men has virtually disappeared in the United States; either is correct for business uses. The use of "loan" as a verb in other connections, however, is less approved, although it cannot be condemned as illiterate.

ADJECTIVES

I. *Pronominal*

1. I was attacked by one of *those* huge police dogs. (32: established)

The votes of the judges clearly place this among acceptable colloquialisms.

2. Harry was a little shaver about *this* tall. (83: established)

Over 75 per cent of the judges classified this expression as cultivated colloquial English.

3. Don't get *these* kind of gloves. (167: disputable)

The linguists ranked this higher than did any other group of judges. The editors placed it, by unanimous consent, at the very bottom of the list of usages; the English and speech teachers rated it nearly as low. Evidently this expression is not at present acceptable as cultivated English in the United States. See also Verbs IV, item 1.

II. *Faulty Forms*

A light *complected* girl passed. (215: illiterate)

This expression was almost unanimously condemned.

ARTICLES

1. *A Tale of Two Cities* is *an* historical novel. (1: established)

Two or three judges remarked that this expression is archaic or old-fashioned. It is distinctly literary, as opposed to colloquial—out of forty-six judges, only ten rated it lower than 1.[4] See also *a orange*.

2. There was *a* orange in the dish. (218: illiterate)

This was one of the few expressions on either ballot on which the vote of the judges was unanimous. There was not one vote for including this form among usages in any way allowable. Contrast *an historical novel*, above.

ADVERBS

I. *Double Negatives*

1. We have*n't but* a few left. (143: disputable)

Here again the English teachers are more severe than the linguists. The locution is not, however, generally approved by either group.

2. I *can't help but* eat it. (153: disputable)

Comments by linguists:
"I mark this 4, but I suppose it may be 1; I could not feel sure without actual search."

"Very common in England and America and grammatically formed."

"I have been studying for forty years the use of *help* in elliptical construction in the sense of *avoid*. 'I couldn't *help* (do anything) but laugh.' *Help* in this meaning is common apart from its use with the

---

[4] This is but one of a number of expressions among the "established usages" which might be called *hyper-urbanisms*—artificial, trite, pedantic, or stilted attempts at correctness.

infinitive: 'I can't *help* it.' The Oxford Dictionary recognizes the construction with the infinitive as grammatical, but remarks that the infinitive is rare, now being replaced by the gerund. The editor was not wide awake when he made the remark. The gerund is the usual form after *help,* but when the conjunction *but* is used the old infinitive construction is very common in the best writers of England and America. I have a large collection of examples from good authors. I shall publish these materials some day."

The Oxford Dictionary cites Hall Caine: "She could not help but plague the lad." The New International and Century Dictionaries definitely accept the expression.

Only the authors placed this expression as low as did the linguists, who were evenly divided between approval and condemnation. Apparently many cultivated people still have a preference for the gerund construction here, but the expression as given cannot be called definitely wrong.

3. I have*n't hardly* any money. (189: illiterate)

A linguist who condemns this says: "But 'I haven't any money, hardly,' would be colloquially acceptable."

Another, also disapproving, says: "But a reguliar idiom in my speech!"

A British linguist remarks: "Sets my teeth on edge, like 'Ere he had scarcely begun . . .' (Burroughs, *Tarzan of the Apes*); 'Hardly had he finished, than . . .' (Sir Edmund Gosse, *Father and Son,* incredible though it may appear)."

With very little disagreement among the various groups of judges, this expression is disapproved for use by educated people.

II. *Adjectives Used as Adverbs*

1. Our catch was *pretty* good. (43: established)

Of forty-eight judges, only one listed this expression as illiterate. Most of the rest placed it among cultivated colloquialisms.

2. That's a dangerous curve; you'd better go *slow*. (56: established)

15 per cent of all the judges approved this as formal literary English; the same proportion condemned it as illiterate (but only 4 of

27 linguists); the rest approved it as colloquial. The Standard, New Int., and N. E. D. all approve *slow* as an adverb.

3. Drive *slow* down that hill! (82: established)

Comments, by judges:
"Might be heard in an excited moment—would hardly be written without coming under class 4."
"It is probably being driven at, but slowly."
"When referring to auto driving the -*ly* is almost universally dropped."

A large majority of judges approved this as good colloquial English, except among the business men and authors. The reason for its being ranged lower than "you'd better go slow" (above) is perhaps best stated in this comment by one of the linguists: "I have marked this 4, though *slow* of course is used properly enough as an adverb—as *go slow* is a commonly accepted informal expression. Followed by a *down* or an *up*, however, I believe one must use *slowly*."

4. My father walked very *slow* down the street. (89: established)

Three of the linguists classify this expression as illiterate. One of them says: "But *go slow* or *drive slow* is good English." Another remarks: "*Walk slow* is good English; followed by a phrase, as here, it is uncultivated."

A linguist who approved the expressions says: "*Slow* and *slowly* give different senses."

Among these distinctions, apparently based squarely in considerations of euphony, the fact emerges that "slow" is safely established as an adverb.

5. He moves mighty *quick* on a tennis court. (69: established)

Though the English teachers rate this considerably lower than do the linguists, a large majority of both groups of judges approve the use of "quick" as an adverb in this context as cultivated colloquial English.

6. Will you go? *Sure.* (133: disputable)

No judge approved this as formal literary English, but a majority of both groups considered the expression as valid in the informal conversation of educated people. It is clearly better independently used than directly modifying a verb or adverb. See next item.

7. It *sure* was good to see Uncle Charles. (176: disputable)

A British authority says that this expression is "impossible in England." Another linguist, who condemns the form, adds, "but in Milton's prose once upon a time!"

"Sure" has not gained approval as a directly modifying adverb.

8. John didn't do so *bad* this time. (157: disputable)

50 per cent of the linguists, and over 35 per cent of the teachers, considered the expression good usage in colloquial English.

9. Yes, our plan worked just *fine*. (165: disputable)

A British linguist says: "Not English except to imitate Americans."

The N. E. D. calls this adverbial use of *fine* "obsolete except dialectal" and gives 1890 as the date of the latest recorded usage.

A small majority of linguists condemned this expression as uncultivated; a large majority of English teachers considered it good as informal English for educated people.

10. If I asked him, he would *likely* refuse. (156: disputable)

Linguists and dictionaries agree that this expression is American or Scottish, as opposed to British, and it is probably acceptable colloquially in those countries. Only the editors placed this expression lower than did the linguists; the other judges assigned it a position near the established usages.

11. It's *real* cold today. (178: disputable)

Comments by judges:

"I have found this provincially on well-bred tongues."

"A little playful."

"Is heard in England, but more colonial or U. S."

Standard Dictionary: "Colloq. U. S.; an erroneous use."

New English Dictionary: "Loosely in later use (chiefly U. S. or Scot)."

Apparently "really," "very," or "extremely" are more acceptable than "real" in expressions like this.

12. **The engine was hitting *good* this morning. (190: illiterate)**

A British linguist says: "Impossible in England."
The judges' vote was over five to one for placing this expression among illiterate usages.

13. **He did *noble*. (226: illiterate)**

The judges unanimously consigned this expression to the class of illiterate usages. But see also *bad, fine, good, quick, real, slow, sure.* Note that these monosyllabic adjectives, except *good*, fall in the disputable or accepted usage categories.

III. *Misuse of Very*

The man was *very amused*. (147: disputable)

"The borderline between the fully naturalized adjective (*interesting, amusing, tired, surprised,* etc.), and the participle is very difficult to determine." (British linguist)
"The use of *very* with past participles has become more common, but *very amused* would not be used by most good speakers." (British linguist)
"I do not like *very amused*. There seems to be a touch of shadowy elegance about that which can be justified no more than the carrying of a stick or the wearing of spats." (British linguist)
"I don't like this but it seems to be good British English." (British linguist)
"Not used. Add *much* and it might go as colloquial." (Editor)
"I have seen *very* plus the past participle in letters of a highly educated English university man (and frequently elsewhere in England since)." (Linguist)
"Spreading rapidly. *Much amused* sounds pompous—or facetious. So I say 'very much amused,'—I *think*. (Perhaps I say 'very amused' without knowing it)." (British linguist)
This is an instance where experts disagree. Nearly 10 per cent of the judges voted that the expression is good literary usage; about

30 per cent considered it acceptable as colloquial; the remainder condemned it. Probably careful speakers will avoid it, but it cannot be called a solecism, nor can its extirpation be made a basic element of school courses in English.

IV. *Doubtful Adverbs*

1. He is *kind of silly*, I think. (134: disputable)

The dictionaries all list this expression as colloquial.
Comments by linguists:
"Indispensable."
"Bad—but 'sort of silly' would be acceptable, and perfectly logical."
"I recognize that *kind of* has come into bad repute, but this is because our grammarians have been men unacquainted with the history of English. For many centuries *kind of* has been an adjective element and is still widely felt as an adjective. It ought to be rescued from the false feeling that has become associated with it from reading our English grammars. This consideration weighs with me! No literary substitute takes its place. We always feel the literary substitute as inadequate. Then, what shall we do with *what kind of* if we condemn *kind of?* Everybody who speaks English says 'What kind of trees are those?' Then, the question of the adverb *kind of* arises. We surely need it. *Kind of* used as an adjective led to the use of *kind of* as an adverb, just as in general an adjective can be used as an adverb."

The judges were nearly equally divided as to the classification of this expression. While it cannot be dismissed as illiterate, it probably is not altogether a safe usage for cultivated speech. Many will prefer *somewhat*.

2. I *felt badly* about his death. (79: established)

A few of the linguists condemned this as "pedantic"; others approved the expression as appropriate to formal, literary English; the majority of all the judges classified it as an acceptable colloquialism.

3. He *most* always does what his wife tells him. (175: disputable)

Here the English teachers were more lenient than the linguists; the judgment of both, however, would place this expression low among disputable usages. See also Pronouns VI.

4. My experience on the farm helped me *some,* of course. (177: disputable)

Dictionaries classify this expression as U. S. (and probably provincial English) dialect. A small majority of the judges would approve it as colloquial; its position is dubious.

5. Well, that's *going some.* (139: disputable)

British linguists agree that this expression is not heard in England. Linguists are about evenly divided on this expression; English teachers do not regard it so leniently. It cannot be said to be accepted.

V. *Position of Adverb*

1. We *only* had one left. (66: established)

Palmer's *Grammar of Spoken English,* 386, p. 184, states: *"Only* is commonly used in the pre-verbal position."

One of the disapproving linguists says: "The best English writers seem to go out of their way to misplace *only."*

Another linguist comments: "Here I think a difference should be made in writing and conversation, since the tone of the voice always indicates in conversation what is limited by *only.* In this particular phrase, 'we only had one left,' ambiguity is hardly possible. In many cases *only,* even in the best literary style, need not precede what *is* modifies. Compare Arnold's 'Dover Beach':

> And now I only hear
> Its melancholy, long, withdrawing roar.

The propriety of the position of *only* depends entirely upon the phrase in which it is used."

Only two of twenty-seven linguists rated this illiterate. A number of authors, editors, and business men rated it disputable, although in the two groups last named a majority approved it. Apparently instruction should attack ambiguous cases only.

2. Cities and villages are being stripped of all they contain *not only, but* often of their very inhabitants. (158: disputable)

This is exactly the same construction as that below: Woodrow

Wilson's use of it probably influenced a quarter of the judges to approve it as literary English; a majority, however, disapproved, probably owing to the extreme awkwardness of the sentence. For the latter reason, this is scarcely a test case.

3. **His presence was valueless** *not only,* **but a hindrance as well. (179: disputable)**

Comments by linguists:

"A Wilsonian, not an English locution."

"Whether Wilson's use of this expression should be called a rhetorical device or an affectation of peculiarity I don't know; its use by others I should set down purely to affectation."

"Not idiomatic, but not incorrect, I suppose, and certainly not colloquial."

"I have never heard the expression."

"Rather a misarrangement than a solecism."

"I cannot imagine anyone putting *not only* in this position. If put before *valueless* I do not object."

This expression caused considerable confusion among the judges because it seemed not to belong to any of the suggested categories. Twenty judges classed it as 1, thirty-one as 2, and about 150 as 4.

Apparently Woodrow Wilson's repeated use of it has not established it as cultivated English.

COMPARISON

I. *Further and Farther*

1. **I felt I could walk no** *further.* **(41: established)**

Only the business men and speech teachers place this among disputable usages. The other five groups of judges consider it as established, their rankings ranging from 12 to 28.

All American dictionaries give *farther* and *further* as synonyms. The N. E. D. says: "In standard English the word *farther* is usually preferred where the word is intended to be the comparative of *far,* while *further* is used where the notion of *far* is altogether absent; there is a large intermediate class of instances in which the choice between the two forms is arbitrary."

Comments by British linguists:

"The effort to make a distinction between *farther* and *further* is still unsuccessful."

" 'I could walk no further' seems quite *wrong* to me, but not vulgar, simply wrong."

" 'He went further than I' (went on beyond the point I went to)— 'He went farther' (had a longer walk)—seems quite a natural distinction to me, though it was probably pedantry with my father, as I don't seem to hear it from other people."

Apparently if there is any distinction between "farther" and "further," it is still too subtle for even experts to be sure of what it is.

2. **This is *all the further* I can read. (202: illiterate)**

Dictionaries do not recognize this expression, and most of the judges rated it as uncultivated.

II. *Superlative Used for Comparative*

Of two disputants, the *warmest* is generally in the wrong. (141: disputable)

(This is the title of one of Lamb's "Popular Fallacies.")

Comments, by linguists:

"Illiterate; though I would differentiate by the comparative in my own discourse, whereas here the *duality* is definitely affirmed in the speech."

"The use of the superlative of two I find quite generally in the conversation of British novels. Evidently in England the rhetoricians haven't been able to frighten people into avoiding it."

"This use of *warm* not natural to me. Ordinary colloquial use of superlative."

Apparently Lamb's (and other authors') use of expressions similar to this has not rendered it entirely acceptable. The editors are almost unanimous in condemning it; the other groups of judges, while not so severe as the editors, give a majority for classing the expression as uncultivated, though many approve it as colloquial, and there is even a scattering of votes for its approval as literary English (possibly by those aware of its origin).

III. *Worse and Worst*

In the collision with a Packard, our car naturally got the *worse* of it. (144: disputable)

One of the linguists who condemns this as uncultivated says: "Semi-literate care for logic, with no sense of idiom."

There was a great deal of disagreement among the judges on this expression. 20 per cent of the linguists and 30 per cent of the teachers approved it as formal English, but a majority of both groups condemned it as illiterate.

PREPOSITIONS

I. *Unusual Uses of*

1. A treaty was concluded *between the four powers*. (75: established)

Only the English teachers ranked this higher than did the linguists. Thirty-two judges approved this as formal literary English; eighty approved it as good colloquial English.

In the New Int. Dict., this very sentence (with three powers, instead of four) is given as an example of the proper use of *between* bringing two or more objects severally and individually into the relation expressed.

N. E. D.: "In all senses, *between* has been, from its earliest appearance, extended to more than two. . . . It is still the only word available to express the relation of a thing to many surrounding things severally and individually, *among* expressing a relation to them collectively and vaguely: we should not say . . . 'A treaty among three powers' . . ."

All the evidence available seems to indicate that the use of "between" in such a context as this is perfectly proper. (See also the remarks on the next phrase, "between each bed.")

2. There is a row of beds with a curtain *between each bed*. (155: disputable)

Facetious comment by a British linguist: "This is one of those expressions even the careless probably feel uncomfortable about. I have heard 'between each bed and the next,' 'between every pair of beds' (objectionable, suggests beds in pairs), 'between every two beds.' *I* use 'and the next' because it enables me to say it wrong, and then put it right."

Another linguist remarks: "The only sensible locution."

Authors and editors condemn this expression as illiterate; the other groups of judges are about equally divided as to its reputability. Evidently it cannot be definitely assigned either to the established or to the uncultivated usages.

3. He came *around* four o'clock. (101 : established)

In America, this expression is good colloquial English. In England it is rarely heard.

4. *Under these circumstances* I will concede the point. (20: established)

The standard deviation of ranking among the groups of judges for this item was only 2.62, and only sixteen of more than 200 placed it in class 4.

The expression is evidently perfectly correct.

5. The old poodle was *to no sense* agreeable. (212: illiterate)

This expression, which is from Arnold Bennett's *Old Wives' Tale*,[5] was thought by the compilers of the ballot to be a fresh and meaningful way of putting the idea. Nevertheless, the English teachers would have placed it among the disputable usages, and only one of the linguists approved it even for colloquial English.

II. *Much Disputed Phrases*

1. *As regards the League,* let me say . . . (30: established)

The linguists, the speech experts, and the M. L. A. judges considered this as established; the other groups of judges rated it as

---

[5] The sentence in *The Old Wives' Tale* is: "Fossette was to no sense a pleasant object." It refers to a sick old dog who smelled evilly and was unpleasant to all the senses. Both the compilers of the ballot and the judges (lacking the context) have entirely misread this item, supposing the *to no sense* to mean *in no sense*. The vote is thus valueless.—R. M. W.

disputed. The linguists ranked it 9; the lowest ranking assigned was that of the business men (47).

2. Sitting *in back of* John, he said, "Now guess what I have." (115: disputable)

A British linguist says that this expression is "never used."
This expression cannot definitely be said to be incorrect, but it is not established as a good usage. See also III, 1 in this section.

3. He stood *in front of* the class to speak. (24: established)

With only one exception, all the judges approved this expression as entirely correct. See also III, 1 in this section.

III. *Omitted Prepositions*

1. The catcher stands *back of* the home plate. (45: established)

The following comment, by one of the linguists, illustrates the metaphysical nature of the controversy that sometimes arises over this expression:

"I maintain . . . that there is a distinction of meaning between *back of* and *behind*. It is not invariable, but they are not always synonyms. A tree growing in front of a house might be hidden behind the house to one in the back yard; but it would not then be back of the house. Is *back of* always opposite to *in front of*, whereas *behind* is beyond something from the observer?"

More of the judges approved this as formally correct than condemned it altogether; but the great majority placed it among the cultivated colloquialisms. See also *in front of* and *in back of*.

2. He doesn't do it *the way I do*. (39: established)

This expression is clearly good colloquial English, but roundabout.

3. Jane *was home* all last week. (52: established)

The judges were nearly unanimous in classifying this as an acceptable colloquialism.

4. He never works *evenings* or *Sundays.* (112: disputable)

Comments, by linguists:

"Rather old-fashioned."

"In a Yorkshire manufacturing town this might be heard more generally than in London."

"*May* be heard in England, but I suppose ordinarily U. S."

Nearly three-quarters of the judges approved this expression, and it is probably quite correct in the United States.

5. Sam, who was then in town, was with me *the three or four first* days. (Quoted from Lamb's "Popular Fallacies") (110: disputable)

Although a majority of judges approved this expression, it cannot be placed among the established usages.

IV. *Elliptical Constructions With*

I enjoy wandering *among* a library. (214: illiterate)

This sentence is from De Quincey's "Essay on Style." It is plainly elliptical yet only two English teachers rated it as correct for formal literary use; one linguist approved it for colloquial use; the remainder of the judges (93 per cent) condemned it as uncultivated.

V. *Redundant Use of*

1. We cannot discover *from whence* this rumor emanates. (50: established)

A linguist, who classes this expression as colloquially acceptable, says: "The *from* seems more redundant than ever in the indirect question. *From whence* in other cases might be 1."

English teachers rate this expression rather low; they are almost equally divided between approval and condemnation. The linguists are more liberal, but rather scattered—five marked this 1; seven marked it 2; while four marked it 4. One was uncertain whether it should be 2 or 4.

In spite of considerable uncertainty, it seems that this may safely be classed among established usages.

2. Now just *where* are we *at?* (192: illiterate)

One linguist says: "Acceptable as jocose."
The linguists and English teachers place this lower than do other groups of judges; no group, however, places it higher than rank 74 out of 100 expressions on the ballot.

3. She leaped off *of* the moving car. (182: disputable)

A linguist says: "Not in my vocabulary, but it would be saying too much to call it illiterate."
The New International Dictionary says, "Formerly in good use, and in dial. and vulgar use still."
Not quite one-third of the judges approve this expression as colloquial English. The remainder consider it uncultivated.

CONJUNCTIONS AND CONJUNCTIVE ADVERBS

I. *Disputed Uses of*

1. This hat is *not so* large as mine. (13: established)

The ratings assigned this expression show that it is entirely correct, but see also *not as,* below.

2. He did *not* do *as* well *as* we expected. (26: established)

Only the M. L. A. judges placed this among the disputed usages (rank 49), but the standard deviation of ranks was over 14, showing considerable uncertainty. The mean rank was 18.
One editor says: "I have marked this sentence 2 (colloquial), for the reason that the distinction between the use of *as* and *so* in positive and negative expressions simply is not made, though recommended by careful writers."
An author says: "*So* should be used with the negative but sometimes is awkward."
The use of *as* in this construction is established in cultivated English.

3. This was the *reason why* he went home. (34: established)

One linguist says: " 'The reason why' is all right, even in 1, but 'the reason was because,' though spreading in newspapers, is bad, decidedly."

All the groups of judges regard "reason why" as established, and the great majority place it in class 2 or among colloquial expressions.

4. The real *reason* he failed *was because* he tried to do too much. (80: established)

The opinions of the judges in this instance leave little doubt that the expression is acceptable colloquially.

5. I don't know *if* I can. (60: established)

Thirty-one from among forty-eight judges approve this as colloquial. The remainder are divided between approval as literary English and condemnation as illiterate. The latter demand *whether* in this sentence.

6. *Either* of these *three* roads is good. (123: disputable)

Standard Dictionary: "*Either* is sometimes used loosely for *any,* referring to a larger number than two."

N. E. D.: "Sometimes equals *each* (of more than two things)."

Comments:

"This does not *sound* illiterate to me, but always looks so!" (Linguist)

"I should *say* this, but I doubt if I should commit it to paper, even in an intimate letter!" (Linguist)

"If we had a satisfactory substitute for the word *either* when we speak of a choice of more than two things, I should not classify this as colloquially acceptable. Of course, the word *any* is satisfactory except that it has so many uses, whereas the word *either* implies choice and for that reason seems to me to be permissible even when this choice is between more than two." (Business man)

"*Either* of more than two does not seem to be in sufficient use to warrant its inclusion as literary English. Yet it does not specifically belong to any of the other groups. *Any* or *any one* seems to serve well enough. Yet many of the best writers have used *either* in this sense." (Linguist)

Although eighteen of twenty-nine linguists approved this expression, among the other judges there was a majority who condemned it as uncultivated. Although it is not definitely among expressions proscribed by usage, it should probably be avoided on the principle that where usage is divided, one is more comfortable on the conservative side. This principle, however, probably does not justify drill to establish the conservative form.

II. *Omission in Double Construction*

He could write *as well* or better *than* I. (119: disputable)

A linguist, in criticizing the categories as indicated on the ballot (see p. 67, above), says: ". . . It seems to me that there are a number of usages which are not in 2, and yet should not be put in 4. I mean usages that arises inadvertently when there is some complexity or difficulty, or lack of forethought in speaking. I cite the above case. The speaker runs on and adds *better* to *as well* and then is in difficulties. If he is writing he can change the order, but in speaking he must make the best of it."

Other comments:

"The second *as* is understood. There is a double comparison and I believe the omission of *as* and the use of the word *than* in such a case is justified. I have, therefore, classed it as 2." (Business man)

"Our language lacks some needed particles for correct conversation —'as well as I, even better than I' is correct but cumbersome." (Linguist)

The fact that the majority of judges approved this expression makes it impossible to say that it is illiterate; the consensus of opinion, however, seems to be that it is awkward, and to be avoided.

III. *Preposition Used as Conjunction* (like *and* as)

1. We don't often see sunsets *like* they have in the tropics. (180: disputable)

A British linguist remarks: "I think I say 'like the ones they have' (I am a schoolmaster). But the other doesn't sound vulgar to me."

A decided majority of judges condemned this expression as uncultivated, although there were enough votes for acceptance to prevent its being placed among indisputably illiterate usages.

2. It looked *like* they meant business. (185: disputable)

A linguist remarks: "The popular instinct in this and analogous uses of *like* is sound; it is more distinctive and clearer than *as*."

This expression found acceptance among only a quarter of the judges. Although not so definitely reprehensible as the usage in the section headed "uncultivated usages," it is probably incorrect.

3. Do it *like* he tells you. (186: disputable)

A British linguist says: "I rate this as good colloquial English— good literary English where clause-verb is suppressed; e. g. 'Roared like a bull.' Where *like* means definitely 'in the very manner' I should rather say 'Do it the way he tells you,' or even 'Do it how he tells you,' though I feel the latter (not the former) to be doubtful—children's English.

"When I use *like* it is rather, so to speak, appositional. 'I ran away of course, like you did' (the same thing which you did).

"When the clause-verb is omitted, everyone uses *like* (even the blithering purists—not realising, with their usual ignorance, what they are doing). 'He drank like a fish.' ('He drank *as* a fish' would mean, of course, when he was a fish.) So that one is forced, of course, to say, 'He danced like a child' since 'as a child' would mean 'when he was.' Meredith says 'threading it with color, like yewberries the yew.' "

Another linguist says: "In some other connexions *like* as a conjunction may be 2." This linguist marked the above expression 4; he marked item two 2 *or* 4, and item one he marked 2.

Still another, who marked this 4, says: "I dare say we shall have to accept this too before long."

The various groups of judges agreed rather closely on this expression. Their vote gives little support to those who consider this use of *like* permissible.

SENTENCE STRUCTURE

I. *Comma Splice*

This book is valueless, that one has more to recommend it.[6] (35: established)

There was no other item on Ballot I that occasioned more uncertainty and disagreement than did this one. It is placed in this section of established usages because the linguistic experts rated it

---

[6] See also conclusions in the punctuation study in *Current English Usage*, p. 21 ff.

high—twenty-two approving as against five who disapproved. No other group of judges was so lenient; only a small majority approved it. It is worth noting that the English teachers placed this lower than did any other group, ranking it as 68 out of the hundred items. This is perhaps due to their having found by experience that the comma blunder is almost impossible to eliminate if even defensible exceptions, like this, are allowed.

A further reason for disagreement among judges for this item probably lies in the fact that the sentence, as it stands, with two clauses in series, represents a different sort of problem from such an expression as "The room was too cold, consequently we had to adjourn." If the latter had appeared on the ballot, it is possible that many more judges would have agreed in condemning it.[7]

II. *Redundant* He

My Uncle John, *he* **told me a story. (199: illiterate)**

A linguist points out: "For longer sentences this construction is common in the best literary use from King Alfred on."

In the sentence here given, this redundance is not in good use.

III. When *in Definitions*

Intoxication is *when* **the brain is affected by certain stimulants. (129: disputable)**

It is probably their weariness of hearing this day after day in the classroom that caused the English teachers to vote nearly four to one for inclusion of this expression among uncultivated usages. The linguists were much more lenient, a majority regarding the locution as admissible in colloquial English.

IV. I Read Where

I read in the paper *where* **a plane was lost. (161: disputable)**

A number of judges considered this expression to be good colloquial English, but the majority would place it among uncultured usages.

---

[7] Mr. George Summey, Jr., in his study of punctuation (*Modern Punctuation*), pp. 79–81, says: "In general, the comma is sufficient only when supported by series, correlation, parallel form, climax, a common modifier, or the momentum of the paragraph. . . . With no link work between successive statements the comma is too light unless supported by special circumstances of structure or momentum."

V. *Incoherent Phrasing*

1. **Factories were *mostly* closed on election day. (68: established)**

The linguists were nearly unanimous in approving this expression; half the English teachers condemned it.

A majority of all the judges, then, consider this good colloquial English. See also *most anybody,* in the section on pronouns.

2. ***Say,* do you know who that is? (151: disputable)**

Linguists say that this expression is not heard in England. In the United States it is a dubious usage. Many people seem to feel that, in special circumstances, *say* as a form of address is impertinence, and condemn it.

BARBARISMS AND IMPROPRIETIES

1. **I wish he *hadn't of* come. (221: illiterate)**

This expression is indubitably illiterate.

2. **If John *had of* come, I needn't have. (224: illiterate)**

This expression has no standing in current usage. See also *hadn't of,* above.

3. ***Hadn't* you *ought* to ask your mother? (222: illiterate)**

All of the linguists, and most of the second jury, regard this locution as illiterate.

4. **I've no doubt *but what* he will come. (94: established)**

A large majority of the judges approved this expression as acceptable colloquial English, in spite of the purists' violence of censure.

5. ***Reverend Jones* will preach. (196: illiterate)**

While the linguists condemned this locution by a majority of four to one, the majority among the English teachers was only two to one. Taking either judgment as a standard, however, this is not an acceptable form.

6. They went *way* around by the orchard road. (103: established)

A British linguist says that this expression is "impossible in England."

Thirty-eight of the forty-eight judges approve the expression as acceptable in informal speech.

7. *That there* rooster is a fighter. (211: illiterate)

The judges were practically unanimous in rating this expression as illiterate.

IDIOMS AND COLLOQUIALISMS

1. It *behooves* them to take action at once. (6: established)

Nearly twice as many judges of all categories placed this expression in 1 as placed it in 2 and 4 together. One linguist calls it "antiquated," another called it "hackneyed." An author calls attention to its use by Shakespeare, Ben Jonson, and Emerson. There was more unanimity of opinion among the seven groups of judges on this than on almost any other item, the standard deviation among the ranks assigned being only 1.46.

This appears to be one of the few expressions belonging distinctly to the literary and formal, rather than the spoken and informal, language.

2. I *had rather* go at once. (7: established)

Several judges pointed out that in speech *had rather* is so pronounced (e. g. *I'd rather*) as to be indistinguishable from *would rather*.

The linguists ranked this as second among the hundred expressions on Ballot I, but when the other judges' rankings are taken into account, the mean rank sinks to 16, with a standard deviation among ranks of over 14. This shows considerable disagreement among the judges as to the exact place this item deserves to occupy. However, each group of judges, except the authors, rated this high enough to give it a place among the established usages.

3. You *had better* stop that foolishness. (10: established)

Every group of judges except the business men accepted this as fully established. Linguists, editors, and English teachers rated it highest.

4. My position in the company was satisfactory from every *point of view*. (14: established)

The judges were nearly unanimous in rating this as entirely correct.

5. My *viewpoint* on this is that we ought to make concessions. (67: established)

A British linguist remarks that this expression is "not used except jocosely."
There is considerable uncertainty manifested in the judges' placement of this; but the great preponderance of expert opinion approves it as a good colloquial usage.

6. He toils *to the end that* he may amass wealth. (15: established)

There was great unanimity of opinion about this expression, no group of judges ranking it lower than 5 out of the 100 expressions on the ballot. Over half the judges classified it as belonging to formal literary English. One or two remarked that it was rarely heard colloquially.

7. *In the case* of students who elect an extra subject, an additional fee is charged. (16: established)

Linguists says: *"Trite but sound";* "I dislike this, but because it is stylistically bad rather than that it is grammatically incorrect."

8. *I for one* hope he will be there. (18: established)

This expression was almost unanimously approved as cultivated colloquial English.

9. You may ask *whomsoever* you please. (22: established)

A large majority of the judges approved this as formal literary English. A few condemned it on the ground that it was too stilted.

10. The women were *all dressed up*. (33 : established)

Nearly all the judges rate this as an acceptable colloquialism.

11. Take two *cups* of flour. (36 : established)

The judges considered that the constant use of this expression in standard works on cookery had established it as cultivated colloquial and informal usage.

12. We have made some progress *along these lines*. (44 : established)

Only one judge condemned this as illiterate; the expression is, however, not fully approved, as witness these comments, by linguists:

"I dislike this, but rather because it is stylistically bad than because it is grammatically incorrect."

"A cant-phrase; slovenly argot of the loose-minded and semi-literate."

"Avoided by the cultivated, but not illiterate."

13. *In hopes of* seeing you, I asked . . . (61 : established)

The linguists gave a large majority for approval of this expression. The English teachers would place it among disputed usages, demanding *hope* instead of *hopes*.

14. I didn't speak to my uncle by long distance; I couldn't *get through*. (84 : established)

This is a peculiarly British usage. About 25 per cent of the judges classified the expression as "technical." Most of the rest approved it as acceptable colloquially. Cf. the American usage, below.

15. Haven't you *got through* yet? (97 : established)

(See also "I couldn't get through," above.)

Both the Standard and the New English Dictionaries define the phrase, without comment, *"get through with,* to complete." The New Int. Dict. gives it as colloquial.

The expression puzzled some of the British judges, one of whom says: "If on the telephone, ordinary; if equivalent to *finished,* not

English." In England the expression could only mean, "Is your telephone connection completed?"

There is a clear majority for this as good colloquial American.

16. It is now *plain and evident* why he left. (92: established)

In each group of judges, there are some who approve this tautological expression as formal literary English, and others who condemn it as illiterate. There are still, however, a majority who classify it as cultivated colloquial usage.

17. My *folks* sent me a check. (100: established)

All the other groups of judges ranked this higher than did the linguists.

Standard Dict.: "Widely used colloquially in spite of the drawing-room fastidiousness of some writers."

New Int. Dict.: "*Folk* is now somewhat archaic; *folks* is commonly considered colloquial."

N. E. D.: "*folks* 4 pl.—The people of one's family, parents, children, relatives."

An American editor writes: "I have rated this 1 (formally correct), thus displaying a good deal of hardihood. Whatever may be the usage in England, in America the expression 'his people' does not ring true. It is either upstage, or contains a covert sneer. No one ever uses the phrase 'my people.' Perhaps the best way in 'literary English' is to sidestep such a phrase altogether."

This is evidently acceptable as colloquial.

18. I *can't seem to* get this problem right. (121: disputable)

A British linguist says: "Not English. Englishmen would use *don't*."

A decided majority of the judges approved this expression as good colloquial usage, but there were enough who condemned it to make its status doubtful.

19. Do you *wish* for some ice cream? (128: disputable)

Remarks by linguists:

"Waitresses' English."

"Modern but now widely used by good authors."

"Not classable, unidiomatic except in special circumstances."

The vote of the English teachers would have placed this among the established usages; the linguists are about evenly divided between approval and condemnation.

20. Trollope's novels have already begun to *date*. (132: disputable)

Dictionaries do not give this verb in this sense. Linguists disagree widely: witness these comments:

"I do not know what this means."

"Literary jargon."

"Critics' slang, perfectly good, even poetic."

"*Date*, for example, is slang, in the strict sense of that term, and a piece of slang that I personally dislike; but while I should certainly not class it as 'cultivated colloquial English,' I hesitate to call it 'vulgar English' and so put it in the same category with 'He won't leave me come in.'"

"Common slang among supposedly cultivated critics now!"

Perhaps this expression should be listed among those justified as technical. The judges approved it, condemned it, and listed it as technical, in nearly equal numbers.

21. It was *good and cold* when I came in. (142: disputable)

Of this expression, linguists say:

"Uncultivated; if *nice* were substituted for *good* I would assign this to 2 (cultivated colloquial usage)."

"This is used widely in my section; I marked it 2; probably it could be marked 1."

"This seems to me idiomatic—*good* probably in the sense of *approaching perfection, thoroughly*."

Speech teachers place this among established usages; the other judges classify it as disputable. We are certainly not justified in considering this expression as definitely bad and to be stamped out.

22. The British look at this differently *than* we do. (168: disputable)

A British linguist remarks, somewhat heatedly: "Good as literary or formal (but wrong for colloquial use). '*From, to, than,* all in best authors'—Concise Oxf. Dict. *Differs* plus dative (Tacitus and elsewhere. Tell the purists Tacitus was a Roman historian and Latin was his native language). *Different: unlike. Like to* is a literary usage; why not *unlike to?* The reference to *differ* is as superficial as most puristic rubbish (speaking dispassionately). The logical analogies of *opposite to, contrary to, dissimilar to,* would never occur to these boneheads. However, there are a number of cases where *different to* can mean something different. E. g. 'He is quite different to me' (He behaves towards me quite differently). So that there is a fairly sound non-purist reason for *different from,* and I try to say it. *Different than* is good formal English, but in colloquial English I think one would say *differently to us* (*or from us*), rather than *than we do.*"

Another linguist says: "Continued observation has convinced me that *different than* is in the best of colloquial and literary use, in spite of the purists. In many cases *from* is decidedly awkward."

This expression has an astonishing range in judges' placements. The business men ranked it 20 out of 102; the linguists, 73, with the other groups distributed in between. Over 15 per cent of the judges approved it as formal English, while about 50 per cent condemned it as illiterate. In short, where experts disagree so widely, it will be unsafe for others to be dogmatic about the standing of this expression.

Changes in Definition and Use of Words

1. Why *pursue* a vain hope? (3: established)

This expression was almost unanimously approved, a large majority of judges placing it among expressions appropriate to formal or literary English.

2. The defendant's case was *hurt* by this admission. (17: established)

A large majority of the judges approved this as cultivated colloquial English; not one condemned it.

3. The honest person is to be *applauded*. (23: established)

Votes of the judges were nearly equally divided as approving this expression as formal or as colloquial English.

4. We *got home* at three o'clock. (27: established)

This expression was placed in class 1 by thirty-eight judges; 159 placed it in class 2.

This expression is clearly good English for colloquial, rather than literary, use. The business of English teachers so far as usage is concerned is evidently to strive to establish cultivated colloquial usage; so there is no reason why any teacher should waste time in trying to suppress this or any other good colloquial expression.

5. I've absolutely *got* to go. (54: established)

The linguists rated this highest, the business men lowest. Eleven out of fifty English teachers condemned the expression—perhaps a survival of the admonitions they received when they were in grade or normal school training. The N. E. D. lists it as "recent colloquial." Some British judges considered it an American locution.

One linguist says, "Acceptable if it means 'am compelled by authority or circumstances.' " Another says, "Acceptable if it means 'can't resist inclination.' "

This is an acceptable colloquialism.

6. I have *got* my own opinion on that. (87: established)

Standard Dict.: "Colloquial."
New Int. Dict.: "Pleonastic."
N. E. D.: "In familiar language."

A linguist remarks: "Quite different in meaning from 'I have my own opinion.' 'He has black eyes,' but 'He's *got* a black eye.' "

Linguists rank this highest, business men, lowest. There is a clear majority for approval as colloquial.

7. *Leave* me alone, or else get out. (140: disputable)

The authors, in most cases the most meticulous among the judges, rated this expression higher than did most of the other groups.

According to the New English Dictionary this expression is synonymous with "let me alone" and is quite accepted. This is confirmed by the judgment of the British linguists in the present study; their composite rank for it is 2.1. Contrast with next item.

8. He won't *leave* me come in. (217: illiterate)

British linguists reject this expression as unfamiliar to them; one says that it is heard in Irish dialects. About 98 per cent of the judges disapproved it. Contrast *leave me alone,* above.

9. *In this connection,* I should add . . . (8: established)

Comments:
"I dislike this, but rather because it is stylistically bad than because it is grammatically incorrect."
"Trite but sound."

10. He has no fear; nothing can *confuse* him. (28: established)

Some judges suggested that perhaps the word "confuse" was ill-chosen; the majority approved the expression as correct.

11. I *drove* the car around the block. (38: established)

This was almost unanimously approved as cultivated colloquial English.

12. The New York climate is *healthiest* in fall. (40: established)

No linguist disapproved the expression; about one-third of the English teachers, probably influenced by the condemnation visited on this construction by most handbooks and rhetorics, condemned it. The preponderance of opinion is clearly in favor of its approval as cultivated colloquial English, the handbooks to the contrary notwithstanding.

13. One is not *fit* to vote at the age of eighteen. (42: established)

Here the two groups of judges agreed that this expression is perfectly acceptable colloquial English.

14. I can hardly *stand* him. (51: established)

A linguist says: "Here the rest of the context must be considered. 'Stand him' strikes me as general, but not cultivated colloquial;

while 'Few can stand prosperity' is undoubtedly good colloquial."

A very large majority of the judges approve this as cultivated colloquial usage.

15. There are some *nice* people here. (57: established)

N. E. D.: "In common use from the latter part of the 18th century as a general epithet of approval or commendation."

A business man says: "I think the word *nice* is decidedly overdone. On the other hand, I classify this as 2 because it seems to me justified by usage."

A linguist says: "I am so accustomed to hearing well bred people use *nice* that I can hardly escape using it in formal writing; I expect to see the word rated 1."

Another: "I confess a personal liking for *nice*. I do not see why *exactly* or *precisely* may not be used in the sense of *exquisite* when applied to human beings or highly organized objects. I believe that the word *nice* has a future."

The judges of all groups displayed practical unanimity in approving this use of the word "nice" as cultivated colloquial English.

16. His attack on my motives made me *peevish*. (64: established)

It is interesting to note that nearly one-third of the judges approved this expression as appropriate to formal literary English, while one-seventh of them condemned it as illiterate. About one-half classified it as colloquial.

This is clearly established as acceptable English.

17. He worked with much *snap*. (71: established)

Only two judges approved this as formally correct English; most of the remainder, however, considered it as good colloquial usage.

18. This room is *awfully* cold. (72: established)

One linguist says: "I say this, but I think I never write it." His opinion is evidently concurred in by most of the judges, for only 4 approve the expression as formally literary, whereas 183 approve it as colloquial. 30 condemn it as illiterate. Dictionaries disagree, some regarding it as slang, others as colloquial. It probably belongs among those expressions which are emerging from slang into the lighter levels of cultivated speech, and is certainly not worth trying to eliminate from the speech of school children.

19. I have a *heap* of work to do. (78: established)

About one-third of the English teachers classified this expression as illiterate; the other two-thirds, together with all but one of the linguists, approved it as good colloquial usage.

20. He made a *date* for next week. (88: established)

All but two of the linguists approved this expression as acceptable colloquially; nearly half the English teachers condemned it. The expression seems to have emerged from the level of slang to that of accepted informal speech.

21. *Can* I be excused from this class? (96: established)

In order to keep the scheme of classification consistent, this is placed among the established usages on the basis of the rating of the linguists, more than three-quarters of whom approved the expression as colloquial. Its position here is, however, made somewhat dubious by the much lower ratings bestowed by the other groups of judges.

Comments by linguists:

"If the speaker means *may,* this is illiterate. The question might be one of possibility."

"*Can* is often condemned, but is common in our best writers."

Probably the fitness of this expression is a matter of taste, rather than usage. But it cannot be listed as vulgar or uncultivated in the face of the large number of judges who recognize its frequent use by cultivated people.

22. Is your insurance sufficient *coverage* for your house? (107: established as technical)

This was the only expression on either ballot which was unqualifiedly classified as technical by the judges. As such, and in its own field, it is entirely correct usage.

23. That clock must be *fixed*. (108: disputable)

British linguists remark that this expression is distinctively American; several point out that in England this could only mean "fixed to the wall, or fastened into position." The Standard, New International, and New English Dictionaries all characterize as colloquial the use of the word represented in this sentence. Linguists and members of the M. L. A. ranked this lowest; speech teachers and editors placed it among entirely acceptable expressions.

This expression is evidently not at present safely established, but it cannot be called a solecism.

24. Have you *fixed* the fire for the night? (59: established)

British linguists remark that the verb *fix,* in England, is used only in the sense of *make fast.*

Practically all the judges approve this expression as cultivated colloquial usage, certainly for the United States.

25. The Rock Island *depot* burned down last night. (114: disputable)

The value of the testimony on this expression is probably weakened by the fact that the sentence was not worded so as to make it unmistakable that *depot* referred to a railway station.

All dictionaries give this meaning of the word as being peculiar to the U. S. The judges for the most part agreed, and a large majority (though fewer than 75%) approved it as correct usage.

Comments:

"Incorrect, if depot means railway station." (British linguist)

"Anglicism? My grandmother, English and an actress, always said 'depot.' " (Speech teacher)

"*Depot* seems to have gone out of fashion very rapidly. Twenty years ago everyone used it in my home town without question." (Linguist)

"*Station* is gaining." (Speech teacher)

"This was once good American usage. It is now countrified rather than wrong." (Editor)

Depot is probably still quite correct in the United States, but seems to be going out of fashion.

26. He went *right* home and told his father. (118: disputable)

The dictionaries record no objection to this use of *right;* the N. E. D. gives many citations from English literature to support the usage.

Each group of judges except the linguists and the authors placed this among established usages.

One British linguist says: "Incorrect, if *right* means *straight.*" But another remarks: "Good colloquial usage if it means 'the whole way home.' Although *straight home* means *immediately* (statim) *home, straight* can't be used in this sense in any other connexion, as far as I know. *Straight home* really means 'starting at once *and* taking the shortest route.' "

This is probably entirely correct for informal speech.

27. I *expect* he knows his subject. (120: disputable)

A linguist says: "I hesitate about this. I use it, but against my own convictions."

The Standard and New International dictionaries call this expression "a colloquial solecism." The N. E. D. says: "Now rare in literary use . . . Its misuse is often listed as an Americanism, but is very common in dial., vulg., or carelessly colloquial speech in England."

One-third of the linguists, and about half the other judges, condemn this expression as uncultivated; its standing is at best uncertain.

28. *I guess* I'll go to lunch. (117: disputable)

Standard Dictionary: "A colloquialism, esp. in the northern U. S., but occurring in English literature as early as the 17th century."

N. E. D.: "Colloq. in northern U. S."

Rupert Hughes says: "*I guess* as used in America is classically good English but is offensive to the British who have let it grow obsolete. Galsworthy, Wells, and others simply cannot reproduce our usage of it in their ridiculous efforts at American dialect.

"As I said in a paper quoted in Mencken's *American Language,* we are under no obligation to accept orders from our English cousins about our common heritage, but *I guess* is perilous to use because it arouses controversy instead of understanding."

British linguists say: "Illiterate here; in U. S. acceptable as colloquial." "This strikes me as American. Used facetiously, as such, by English people." "As proper as *I fancy, I imagine, I* think."

Of twenty-three authors, twelve approved this expression as literary English, eleven condemned it as illiterate. A large majority of the remaining judges classified it as acceptable in informal American English. It is probably still safely established in the United States.

29. I *calculate* to go soon. (201 : illiterate)

This is a localism, and is not allowable in general use.

30. That boy's mischievous behavior *aggravates* me. (162 : disputable)

American dictionaries label this expression "colloquial"; the Oxford Dictionary calls it "familiar." The judges are nearly equally divided between approval and condemnation. While not altogether incorrect, it is evidently not established as a cultivated colloquialism.

31. It is *liable* to snow tonight. (170 : disputable)

The Oxford Dictionary supports the expression with many citations from writings from 1682 to 1896.

The fact that nearly as many judges approved this expression as condemned it places it among usages concerning whose correctness nothing positive can be said on either side.

32. They went in *search for* the missing child. (171 : disputable)

Both groups of judges voted about two to one against the inclusion of this expression among permissible usages.

33. John was *raised* by his aunt. (173 : disputable)

Linguists and dictionaries agree that this expression is U. S. dialect, especially in the South and West. English teachers and business men rate it relatively high. While not commonly accepted as educated usage, it cannot be said to be a solecism.

34. **Both leaves of the drawbridge** *raise* **at once. (208: illiterate)**

Although the English teachers rate this expression more leniently than do the linguists, both groups give large majorities for its inclusion among illiterate usages.

35. **The** *party* **who wrote that was a scholar. (198: illiterate)**

A linguist says: "Not classable—strictly correct but unidiomatic."
Nine judges rated this as a technical expression, probably because they felt that it was allowable in legal jargon. As non-technical English, it is not in good standing.

36. **I was pretty** *mad* **about it. (122: disputable)**

A linguist remarks, "Hardly English. English colloquial *sick*."
Standard Dictionary: ". . . archaic in lit. Colloquially, in the U. S., *mad* in this sense is very common, and as a provincialism is not uncommon in England. Its use may be regarded as permissible colloquially when connected with a cause of vexation that is not a person."
N. E. D.: "Now only colloq."
In the U. S. this is probably acceptable in informal discourse.

37. **That will be** *all right,* **you may be sure. (48: established)**

There is practically no disagreement among the judges in classifying this expression as established in cultivated colloquial usage. Only five out of over 200 condemn it as vulgar. Some of those who classed it as colloquial indicated that they believed it would soon belong with literary English.
The N. E. D. gives 1686 as the date of its earliest recorded use, and makes no objections to the form.

DEBATED SPELLINGS

Such *naif* actions seem to me absurd. (148: disputable)

The Standard Dictionary says: "Same as *naive*."
One linguist says: "In English usage naive is employed without

reference to gender. The use of *naif* for *naive* is a purist affectation."
Another remarks: "I have *read* such sentences a few times."

18 per cent of all the judges classified this expression as technical;
the rest were almost evenly divided between the other three classifications—almost as many thought it acceptable for formal literary English as condemned it as illiterate! The expression then, clearly belongs
among disputable usages because there is no agreement as to its
standing.

III

PRACTICAL CONCLUSIONS AS TO GRAMMAR
AND USAGE

What practical conclusions applicable in classroom instruction can be drawn from the findings of this grammatical study? As in the case of punctuation, two lines of procedure suggest themselves: usages upon which the judges strongly agree can be profitably taught; in regard to usages upon which the judges are evenly divided, dogmatism is unjustified. Extensive drill on either form of a divided usage would clearly be a loss of time; and it is equally obvious that no class time should henceforth be wasted in an effort to eradicate any construction here listed as established—no matter what the personal preference of the instructor or the dictum of the adopted text.

Two considerations guide the teacher of composition in his approach to the subject of grammatical usage: first, how near to correctness and clarity he can bring the average language level of his class; and second, what he can do to lift superior students from mediocrity to elegance in their use of English. Where composition classes are sectioned according to language ability, the problem is somewhat simplified, since in superior sections the more illiterate mistakes in sentence structure and usage will not need to be eradicated and stress can be placed on finer points of style. In the mixed class, however, one has constantly to choose between the presentation in group instruction of a standard far more meticulous than can be attained by the average student, or the presentation of a standard attainable by the average but little if at all higher than that already reached by the better students. The wise instructor will probably solve the difficulty by drilling the class upon the requirements to be demanded of the average and either using the superior students as assistants in carrying on this drill, or excusing them entirely from participation therein, and then presenting to them individually or in a separate group the more exacting standards to which he thinks they may attain.[8] Whichever of these methods he adopts, he will certainly in marking themes accept from the average student any usage classed in this study as established or disputable. To the student more skilled in the use of English, he should privately suggest more elegant locutions in place of disputable usages. The superior child capable of reaching distinction in speech or writing deserves such individual instruction as will open up to him the finer manipulation of language. But except in those limited portions of the composition course necessarily devoted to class drill or individual conference on items of grammar and usage, there is little doubt that both average and superior students alike will profit more by attention to the interest and clarity of their oral and written work, to the richness of their observation of life, the soundness of their thought, the organization of their material, and the originality of their expression, than by the most thorough and painstaking usage drill.

Upon the moot question of how far the study of formal grammar can improve the speech habits of our students, the present study throws little light. To the study of grammar itself, however, it makes anew two contributions of major and perennial importance.

In the first place, grammar is seen to be not something final and static but merely the organized description or codification of the actual speech habits of educated men. If these habits change, grammar itself changes, and textbooks must follow suit.

---

[8] *Class Size* in *High School English.* Dora V. Smith, University of Minnesota Press.

To preserve in our textbooks requirements no longer followed by the best current speakers is not grammatical but ungrammatical. It makes of grammar not a science but a dogma.

Many teachers—and, for that matter, most persons who have not specialized in the observation of language ways—conceive of rules in grammar as laws to which language must conform, in the same way that the man in the street conceives of physical laws as governing the behavior of matter. We are accustomed to saying, for instance, that certain laws "govern" the behavior of gases under pressure, and we naturally think of the operation of these laws as being like that of the laws which govern the behavior of a civilized individual in a commonwealth—as something promulgated to regulate action. The physical law is really a statement of how gases have been observed to behave under certain conditions, and the physicist stands ready to change the "law" the moment observation shows this behavior to be in any way different from what he had formerly thought. In the same way, the grammatical rule that the complement of the verb *to be* is always in the nominative case, is also merely a statement of the way people actually write and speak, and the moment people cease to write or speak in this way, this particular "law" of grammar must be changed. In the paragraphs numbered 2 and 3, immediately below, are cited certain apparent violations of the rules of formal grammar which have become so well established in the language of educated people that they are now in reputable usage. The use of the word *violation* in this connection is really highly inaccurate, in the same way that it would be inaccurate to say that a gas's failure to act in the way predicted by Boyles' Law was a violation of that law. We should say, instead, that the statement of the law must be revised so that it would more accurately describe the behavior of the gas.

There are three such tentative general revisions of the grammar of written and spoken English which this study seems to validate.

1. A number of usages entirely in accord with the present rules of formal grammar are apparently avoided by careful speakers and writers because they are regarded as finical or pedantic. Among these [9] are the use of the article *an* with certain words (such as *historical*) beginning with *h;* the strained avoidance of the split infinitive; and insistence upon a formal sequence of *ones* in such a sentence as "One must mind one's manners." These expressions we should not forbid; but we certainly should not encourage their use by dogmatic requirement.
2. There are expressions which are condemned by most handbooks and which are listed among improper usages in the chapters on diction in many school rhetorics but which are nevertheless in frequent use by educated speakers. It might be wise not to assign such chapters to pupils until the acceptability of the expressions has been checked by the findings of this study.[10]
3. Formal grammar is apparently at fault in setting up rigid rules for the case of personal pronouns after *to be* and of the interrogative pronoun *who.*[11]

The second contribution made by this investigation of the study of grammar relates to the principle which apparently guides grammatical change. If the point of view of the judges in reaching their decisions regarding these usages is correct, the governing principle in the use of language, as of punctuation, is clarity of thought. "Which phrasing most accurately expresses the intended meaning?" seems to be their constant question. The usage which does this will be the usage upon which educated persons finally settle and which will thus become grammatical. If meaning is the midwife at the delivery of usage (of which grammar is only the codified description), should not meaning likewise be the governing principle in the teaching of formal grammar? Probably no study is allotted more time and is more barren of results than that from which our grammar schools de-

[9] See index under *hyper-urbanisms.*
[10] See index for *not—as; reason why; none are; healthy* for *healthful; pretty good; back of;* the use of *shall, will, should, would,* etc.; *try and; got to;* the split infinitive; *slow* and other adjective forms used as adverbs (see index under *adverbs*) ; *fix* for *repair;* the position of *only,* etc.
[11] See index under *pronouns, case of.*

rive their name. After five or six years of grammar work in the elementary schools; after endless diagramming (which is but parsing in pictorial reincarnation); after painful memorizing of rules and definitions; and after constant composition of illustrative exercises, many a high school freshman cannot write or speak a decent English sentence. Propose a review of grammar, and the response will be a politely smothered groan. Yet often these same children will enjoy the grammar work incidental to foreign language, and will suddenly awaken to facts about their own tongue which all their study of English grammar never revealed. The reason for this is patent. Although the teaching of other grammars has its vices, it has usually the virtue of being purposeful. Grammar is felt to be an aid to expression in the new language—a way of getting thoughts marshaled and intelligibly put. It is something dynamic, a usable tool.

All too often the teacher of English grammar is not constructive but analytic. Instead of doing something interesting by means of grammar, the pupils are asked to pull the language to pieces and examine its dead fragments. But children are no analysts. They are not interested in pieces; they want moving wholes. The result is that instead of seeing that grammar is merely common sense applied to language to help us express our ideas clearly, children regard it as a jumble of abstract rules, quite meaningless and negligible in every day life. Most of us can recall learning as children from a text still widely employed that a sentence was a thought expressed in words. That was the first and last time thought was mentioned in the book. The rest of the discussion was about words. We named and classified words; we declined and conjugated them; we juggled with their gender; we stuck them together in what we called sentences; we hacked real sentences up into words; we isolated poor shivering little *if*'s and *the*'s and examined them mercilessly in all their nakedness. And we naturally concluded that sentences were mere mosaics plastered together with grammatical cement. That the sentence was a living organism, an indivisible whole, the throbbing body of an interesting thought, never occurred to us.

The whole method of attack was pedagogically wrong. Little brains and little fingers are very much alike; both lack the power of fine manipulation. The baby can grasp a squirming kitten; he fumbles over and drops a tiny bead. But textbooks on grammar are written by grown ups who have at once the power of handling detail and the understanding of wholes, neither of which the child has yet acquired. They present a subject not descriptively as youth demands but analytically as age prefers. They contain the anatomy and not the biology of language. They arrest language instead of putting it in motion.

If it be that some study of grammatical laws is necessary to mature manipulation of language, the study should begin at the other end. The whole sentence should first command attention. Children will be quick to recognize its completeness or incompleteness when they are looking at it as a statement of an interesting thought, a deed performed, a fact noted. If the sentence must be cut up at all, let it be into big thought blocks. If diagramming must be done, let it be the old fashioned sausage-link kind, expressing simply, without hair splitting, the big primary grammatical relations.

There is undoubtedly a place in the curriculum for a thorough study of those grammatical principles which seem to govern all language because they also govern the logic of thought, and hence of its communication. But unless this study *is* a study of logic and not of formal rules; unless this study *does* keep pace with actual usage instead of insisting upon a petrification of principles which reduces the grammar text to a volume of folk lore and curious myths, grammar study can neither change illiterate usage nor produce that mature power over the manipulation of language which a knowledge of fundamental principles gives the scientist or the artist over the manipulation of the materials of his science or his art.

INDEX